THE INFINITE WAY

THE INFINITE WAY

JOEL S. GOLDSMITH

DeVorss Publications
Camarillo, California

The Infinite Way
Copyright © 1947, 1956
By Joel S. Goldsmith

ISBN: 087516-309-2
Thirty-third Printing, 2004

DeVorss & Company, Publisher
P.O. Box 1389
Camarillo CA 93011-1389
w w w . d e v o r s s . c o m

Printed in the United States of America

"The world is not in need of a new religion, nor is the world in need of a new philosophy. What the world needs is healing and regeneration. The world needs people who, through devotion to God, are so filled with the Spirit that they can be instruments through which healing takes place."

■ JOEL S. GOLDSMITH

THE INFINITE WAY

By Joel S. Goldsmith

We are reminded in this book that the great Power necessary to dispel the erroneous conditions which surround us, must be sought within ourselves — and we are shown how it may be accomplished.

We are seeking, as never before, that which will free us from the fears, anxieties and dangers of material living. We know that whatever it is that will give us mental rest and spiritual peace does not lie in the realm of human thought.

We live under the illusion that material forces and human will are great powers until we learn that within our own being there is a spiritual power which dispels this illusion.

There is a "Peace, be still" within our own consciousness which will still every storm in our experience, heal our diseases, lift us above the strife and weariness of human existence.

Our part is to recognize its presence within ourselves and *Let* it fulfill its mission. This universal power of Truth, Life, and Love is ours regardless of which church we attend or what philosophy we follow. It abides at the center of every individual, saint or sinner, awaiting only our recognition.

The awareness that human power does not regulate the sun and stars in the heavens; the crops in the earth, the winging of birds in the air—is sufficient faith to move mountains of discord. No greater faith is necessary.

What must we do to be saved from the ills and terrors of these present days? Let the message of this book fill your consciousness with its spiritual import—and be patient; *Let* the harmonies of spiritual existence unfold from within you and lead you out of the bondage of sense into the promised land of peace.

Joel S. Goldsmith, the author of this book, was a seeker for Truth in all the great religions and philosophies. He devoted many years to the public practice of healing and counselling in all phases of human existence. His unfoldment of the Light Within is well known through his "Letters" which for many years have had wide circulation. "Infinite Way" study groups have been formed throughout the U.S. to study the Goldsmith writings.

Dedicated

to whom this already belongs,

you

CONTENTS

There is no need to run outside
For better seeing,
Nor to peer from a window. Rather abide
At the center of your being;
For the more you leave it, the less you learn.

LAO-TZE

Truth is within ourselves.
There is an inmost center in us all,
Where the Truth abides in fulness; and to know
Rather consists in opening out a way
Whence the imprisoned splendor may escape
Than in effecting entry for a light
Supposed to be without.

ROBERT BROWNING

A God has made His abode within our breast:
when He rouses us, the glow of inspiration warms
us; this holy rapture springs from the seeds of
the divine mind sown in man.

OVID

Most men take a problem, not to themselves, not
into the chambers of their own minds, but to the
first directory of persons whom they can consult.

VALDIVAR

The kingdom of God is within you.

JESUS

AUTHOR'S NOTE

There is a *way* whereby we are able to rid ourselves of sin, sickness, poverty, and the results of wars and economic changes. This way is the exchanging of our material sense of existence for the understanding and consciousness of life as spiritual.

Down the centuries, the sense of man and the universe as being material has resulted in the development of fear for the personal self and national existence. This will continue and become even more intensified as more destructive material forces are discovered. The latest of these forces to be announced is a chemical, one ounce of which, it is claimed, would be sufficient to destroy the entire population of the United States and Canada, and even this is probably not the ultimate of material force. There is no material power to overcome either this or the atomic bomb. There is no hope in matter or material sense. The *way* of security, harmony, and health is through attaining some measure of spiritual consciousness.

The great secret is that despite all belief to the contrary real power, either for good or evil, does not reside in matter or in the material sense of man and the universe. Those who have acquired some degree of spiritual consciousness have proved in that measure the reality of Spirit.

The necessity for giving up the material sense of existence for the attainment of the spiritual consciousness of life and its activities is the secret of the seers, prophets, and saints of all ages. That it is practical is proved today by the healing and regenerating works done by many students of modern schools of practical or scientific Christianity. When the world learns that whatever success has been gained in improving conditions of health, wealth, and security in the lives of these modern followers of ancient teachings has been accomplished solely by the surrender of material sense through the attainment of spiritual consciousness, it may well look up with hope.

The question is, "How does one set about attaining this spiritual consciousness and thereby lose material sense?" The answer is, "Read and study the truths revealed through all ages about the universal Consciousness, Soul or Spirit, and about spiritual creation and its laws. Imbibe the spiritual sense of these revelations."

In this small volume, I have written the spiritual truth as I have gleaned it through over thirty years of study of the major religions and philosophies of all ages, the last fifteen years of which have been spent in the practical application of truth to problems of human existence – problems of health, business, family life, and security.

Be assured inner peace will come as one turns to the spiritual consciousness of life, and an outer calm will follow in one's human affairs. The outer world will conform to the inner awareness of Truth.

The authority for all of this revelation will be you – as you yourself experience this change within and without.

THE INFINITE WAY

PUTTING ON IMMORTALITY

"IN THE BEGINNING was the Word, and the Word was with God, and the Word was God. . . . And the Word was made flesh."

"The Word was made flesh" – but it still is the Word. By being made flesh it does not change its nature, character, or substance. Cause becomes visible as effect, but the essence or substance is still the Word, Spirit or Consciousness.

In this wise, do we understand that there is not a spiritual universe *and* a material world, but rather that what appears as our world is the Word made flesh, Spirit made visible, or Consciousness expressed as idea.

All the error that has existed down the ages is founded on the theory or belief of two worlds, one the heavenly kingdom, or spiritual life, and the other a material world or mortal existence, each separate from the other.

In spite of this sense of two worlds, men have always attempted to bring harmony into the discords of human existence through an attempt, by prayer, to contact this other world, or spiritual realm, and to bring Spirit, or God, to act upon the so-called material existence.

Let us begin with the understanding that our world is not an erroneous one, but rather that the universe in which we live is the realm of reality about which man entertains a false concept. The work of bringing health and harmony into our experience is not, then, getting rid of, or even changing, a mortal material universe, but correcting the finite concept of our existence.

The seeker of Truth begins his search with a problem – perhaps with many problems. The first years of his search are devoted to overcoming discords and healing disease through prayer to some higher Power or the application of spiritual laws or truth to these mortal conditions. The day arrives, however, when he perhaps discovers that the application of truth to human problems either does not "work" or does not work as it once did, or else he finds there is now less of satisfaction and inspiration in his study. Eventually, he is led to the great revelation that mortals put on immortality only as mortality disappears – they do not add immortal spiritual harmony to human conditions. God does not create, nor does He control material affairs. "But the natural [human] man receiveth not the things of the Spirit of God: for they are foolishness unto him: neither can he know them, because they are spiritually discerned."

Are we seeking "the things of the Spirit of God" for some human purpose, or are we really endeavoring to "put off" the mortal in order that we may behold the harmony of the spiritual realm?

While we strive and struggle and contend with the so-called powers of this world, combating sickness and sin or lack, spiritual sense reveals that "My kingdom is not of this world." Only as we transcend the desire to improve our humanhood do we understand this vital statement. When, however, we leave the realm of human betterment, we catch the first glimpse of the meaning of "I have overcome the world."

We have not overcome the world while we are seeking to have less of the world's pains and more of the world's pleasures and profits. And if we are not overcoming the sense of struggle over worldly affairs, we are not entering the realm of heavenly affairs.

"For whatsoever is born of God overcometh the world." Spiritual consciousness overcomes the world – both the pains and pleasures of the world. We cannot accomplish this evangelization of humanhood by mental might or physical power, but by the spiritual sense of existence which all may cultivate through devotion of thought to the things of the Spirit. "For all that is in the world, the lust of the flesh, and the lust of the eyes, and the pride of life, is not of the Father, but is of the world." Here is the guide. Watch your thoughts, aims, and ambitions for just a short while and see if your mind is on your health, the pleasures of the senses, or worldly gain. Then as these worldly thoughts appear, learn to reject them because now we are no longer set on the path of improving our human affairs, but on attaining the spiritual kingdom.

"Love not the world, neither the things that are in the world. If any man love the world, the love of the Father is not in him." Does this sound as if we were becoming ascetic? Do we appear now to be desiring a life apart from the normal, joyous, successful walks of life? Do not be deceived. Only those who have learned to keep their attention on spiritual things have tasted the full joys of home, companionship, and successful enterprise. Only those who have in a measure become centered in God have found safety, security, and peace right in the midst of a war-torn world. Spiritual sense does not remove us from our normal surroundings, nor does it deprive us of the love and companionship so necessary to a full life. It merely places it on a higher level where it is no longer at the mercy of chance or change or loss, and where the spiritual value of the so-called human scene is made manifest.

"Labour not for the meat which perisheth, but for that meat which endureth unto everlasting life . . . For the kingdom of God is not meat and drink; but righteousness, and peace, and joy in the Holy Ghost."

When confronted with any human problem, instead of laboring for an improved human condition, turn from the picture and realize the presence of the divine Spirit in you. This Spirit dissolves the human seeming and reveals spiritual harmony, though to sight this harmony will appear as improved human health or wealth. When Jesus fed the multitude, it was his spiritual consciousness of abundance that appeared as loaves and fishes. When he healed the sick, it was his feeling of the divine Presence that appeared as health, strength, and harmony.

This may all be summed up in Paul's words: "Set your affection on things above, not on things on the earth."

We are living in a spiritual universe, but the finite sense has set a picture before us of limitation. While thought is on the picture before us — "this world" — we are engaged in the constant effort to improve or change it. As soon as we lift our vision — take thought off what we shall eat and drink and wear — we begin to behold spiritual reality which appears to us as improved beliefs, but which really is more-appearing of reality. This more-appearing reality brings with it joys untold here and now, pleasures beyond our wildest imagination and the love of all with whom we come in contact, even the love of those who do not know the source of the new life we have discovered.

"Peace I leave with you, my peace I give unto

you; not as the world giveth, give I unto you."

"Now we have received, not the spirit of the world, but the spirit which is of God . . . Which things also we speak, not in the words which man's wisdom teacheth, but which the Holy Ghost teacheth . . . But the natural man receiveth not the things of the Spirit of God: for they are foolishness unto him: neither can he know them, because they are spiritually discerned."

How often do we go on the rocks on this point! How frequently do we attempt to understand spiritual wisdom with our human intellect! This leads to mental indigestion because we are attempting to digest spiritual food with our educated mentality. It will not work. Truth is not a reasoning process; therefore, it must be spiritually discerned. Truth does not as a rule appeal to our reason, and when it appears to do so, we must search deeply to see if it really is truth. Be suspicious of a truth that seems reasonable.

Jesus, walking on the water, feeding the multitudes with a few loaves and fishes, healing the sick and raising the dead – does all this seem reasonable to you? If the principle underlying these experiences could be understood through reason, all the churches would be teaching it as a present possibility and they would recommend its practice. But this principle is apparent only to spiritual sense, and this cultivated spiritual consciousness can do the things that the Christ has ever done. What was possible to Christ-consciousness in Jesus' time is possible to that same Consciousness now.

We now are engaged in the cultivation of that spiritual sense and we shall succeed in proportion as we relax our mental struggle and become receptive to those things which the Spirit of God teaches. Instead of trying to make Spirit operate upon our human bodies and material affairs, let us learn to disregard these mortal pictures and keep our vision on things above. When we "come down to earth again," we shall find the discords and limitations of sense disappearing and more of reality appearing.

The kingdom of God does not consist of more and better matter, nor does it necessarily include a greater vocabulary of truth. Yet the fruitage of spiritual understanding is greater harmony, peace, prosperity, joy, and more ideal companionships and relationships.

"For this cause also thank we God without

ceasing, because, when ye received the word of God which ye heard of us, ye received it not as the word of men, but as it is in truth, the word of God, which effectually worketh also in you that believe" – understand.

To receive the word of God or spiritual sense, we need to feel rather than reason. This is referred to biblically as receiving the word "in the heart." Note here that the development of spiritual consciousness results in a greater gift of feeling the harmony of being. We understand that neither seeing, hearing, tasting, touching, nor smelling will reveal spiritual truth or its harmonies to us; therefore, it must come through a different faculty, the intuitive faculty which acts through feeling. Heretofore, we have sat down to pray or to meditate and immediately a stream of words and thoughts started to flow. Perhaps we began to affirm truth and deny error. You can see that this is wholly in the realm of the human mind.

In cultivating our spiritual sense we become receptive to thoughts which come to us from within. We become hearers of the Word rather than speakers. We become so attuned to Spirit that we feel the divine harmony of being; we feel the actual presence of God. Having transcended the five physical senses, our intuitive faculty is alert, receptive and responsive to the things of the Spirit, and we begin our new existence as a result of this spiritual rebirth.

Heretofore, we have been concerned with the letter of truth, now only with the spirit of truth. We are not so concerned now with what is truth as with feeling truth. This is accomplished in proportion as we give less thought to the letter and more receptivity to the feel. This word "feel" incidentally, refers also to the awareness, consciousness, or a sense of truth. We are not now speaking truth but receiving truth, and that which we receive in silence we may speak from the housetops with authority.

Spiritual healing is the natural result of a divinely illumined consciousness. We are illumined only as we are receptive and responsive to spiritual illumination.

We misunderstand immortality when we think of it as the immortality of the human personality, or personal sense. Death does not produce immortality or end personal sense, nor does the continuation of human existence mean the attainment of immortality.

Immortality is attained in proportion as personal sense is overcome, whether here or hereafter. As we put off the personal ego and attain the consciousness of our real Self – the Reality of us, divine Consciousness – we attain immortality. And that can be achieved here and now.

The desire to perpetuate our false sense of body and wealth ensnares us into death, or mortality.

The first step in the attainment of immortality is living *out* from the center of our being, as in the idea of unfoldment from within, rather than accretion: It is the *giving* sense rather than *getting;* *being* rather than *attaining.* In this consciousness, there is no condemnation, judgment, hatred, or fear, but rather a continuous feeling of love and forgiveness.

It is not a simple matter to show forth the joy and peace of immortality, because to those intent on preserving their present concepts of being, immortality would appear to be extinction. This is not the case: It is the eternal preservation of all that is real, fine, noble, harmonious, gracious, unselfish, and peaceful. It is *reality* brought to light in place of the illusion of sense. It is the conscious awareness of the infinity of individual being replacing the finite sense of existence.

Selfishness and conceit fall away in the realization of the divinity of our being.

This realization brings forth patience and forbearance with those still struggling in mortal, material consciousness. It is being *in* the world but not *of* it.

SPIRITUAL ILLUMINATION

SPIRITUAL ILLUMINATION enables us to discern the spiritual reality where the human concept appears to be. Spiritual sense discerns the reality of that which is appearing as concept.

The development of spiritual consciousness begins with our first realization that what we are beholding through the senses of sight, hearing, taste, touch, and smell is not the reality of things. Disregarding appearances entirely, the first ray of spiritual illumination brings us hints of the divine, the eternal and immortal. This in turn makes the appearance even less real to us, thereby admitting even greater illumination.

Our progress Spiritward is in proportion to the illumination which enables us to behold more and more of Reality. Because the human scene is entirely a misconception through misperception, any thought of helping, healing, correcting, or changing the material picture must be relinquished in order that we may see the ever-present Reality.

Spiritual illumination comes to us in a measure with our first investigation of truth. We believe that we are seeking good, or truth; whereas the light has begun to shine in our consciousness compelling us to take the steps we have since taken. Every increase of our spiritual understanding was more light appearing and dispelling the darkness of sense. This inflow of illumination will continue until we come to the full realization of our true identity as "the light of the world." Without illumination, we struggle with the forces of the world; we labor for a living; we struggle to maintain our place and position; we compete for riches or honors. Often we war with our own friends and even find ourselves at war with ourselves. There is no security in personal possessions even after the battle to acquire them has been won.

Illumination first brings peace, then confidence and assurance; it brings rest from the world's contests, and then all good flows to us through Grace. We see now that we do not live by acquiring, gaining, or achieving. We live by Grace; we possess all as the gift of God; we do not get our good, because we already have all good. "Son, thou art ever with me, and all that I have is thine."

The pleasures and successes of the world are as nothing compared with the joys and treasures which now unfold to us through spiritual sense. In the light of truth, the greatest earthly happiness and triumph are as nothing, whereas the treasures of Soul have a glory unknown and unfathomed by sense.

Possessing the divine Light within him, man gains his freedom from the world and security from all earthly or human dangers. This period holds terrors and fears for many. The spiritually illumined will recognize that because no good can come or go, that because spiritual activity is always of the nature of fulfillment, that because their illumination has revealed the reality of things, they are anchored in Soul, in God-consciousness, in spiritual peace, security, and serenity.

We will fear no change in the outer picture because the outer is but the reflection of the allness within. Safe in the realization that we are individual though infinite spiritual consciousness embodying all good, we need give no consideration to the evidence of the senses.

Spiritual illumination reveals the harmony of being and dispels the evidence of material sense.

It does not change anything in the universe for this is a spiritual universe peopled with children of God, but the illumination changes our concept of the universe.

This is but the beginning of this vast subject, and while we are discussing it, let us keep thought removed as far as possible from the world of sense and anchored in the conscious awareness of spiritual reality.

Always there have appeared men bearing the divine message of the presence of God and of the unreality of evil: Buddha of India; Lao-Tze of China; Jesus of Nazareth. These and many others brought the light of Truth to men, and always men have interpreted this Light as the messenger, failing to see that what they were beholding as a man "out there" was the light of Truth within their own consciousness.

In worshiping Jesus, men lost the Christ. In devotion to Jesus, men failed to apprehend the Christ. In seeking good through Jesus, men failed to find the omnipresent Christ in their own consciousness.

In every case, the messenger appearing to man is the advent of the Christ in individual consciousness, and when so understood, freedom from personal sense and personal limitation has been attained.

Jesus said, "If I go not away, the Comforter will not come unto you." Was this not clear enough for all to understand? If you do not look away from the personal sense of salvation, mediation, and guidance, you will not find the great Light within your own consciousness.

Spiritual illumination does not come from a person, but from the impersonal Christ, the universal Truth, the illumined consciousness of your Self.

Illumined consciousness dispels the personal sense of self with its problems, ills, age, and failures. It reveals the real Self, the *I* that I am, unlimited, unfettered, untroubled, harmonious, and free. This Selfhood is revealed as we retire within ourselves each day and there learn to "listen" and to watch. Likewise, instead of anxious care about the work of the day or the events of the future, we let the Soul, or our divine Spirit, go ahead of us to smooth and prepare the way; we let this divine Influence remain behind us to safeguard every step from the illusions of sense.

Illumined consciousness always knows that there

is an infinite, all-powerful Presence prospering every act and blessing every thought. It knows that all who touch us on life's highway must feel the benediction of our thought.

When consciousness is afire with Truth and Love, it destroys all sense of fear, doubt, hate, envy, disease, and discord — and this pure consciousness is felt by all whom we meet, and it lightens the load they carry. It is impossible to be "the light of the world" and not dispel the darkness of those about us.

Realize that all the good you experience is the shining forth of your own consciousness even when it appears to come from, or through, some other individual. Recognize every evil appearance as a false perception of harmony and therefore not to be feared or hated, and this will result in the disappearance of the illusion and the showing forth of reality. Only illumined consciousness can look upon an evil appearance and perceive the divine reality. Only the Christ in consciousness can strip error of its seeming reality and rob it of its sting.

Spiritual illumination reveals that we are not mortals — not even human beings — but that we are pure spiritual being, divine consciousness, self-sustaining life, all-inclusive mind. This light destroys the illusions of personal sense.

Illumination dissolves all material ties and binds men together with the golden chains of spiritual understanding; it acknowledges only the leadership of the Christ; it has no ritual or rule but the divine, impersonal, universal love, no other worship than the inner Flame that is ever lit at the shrine of Spirit. This union is the free state of spiritual brotherhood. The only restraint is the discipline of Soul; therefore, we know liberty without license; we are a united universe without physical limits, a divine service to God without ceremony or creed.

The illumined walk without fear — by Grace.

To know that we are the fulfillment of God, that we are that place in consciousness where God shines through, is to be spiritually minded. The realization that every individual is the presence of God, that all that is, is God appearing, is spiritual consciousness. The understanding that what we see, hear, taste, touch, or smell through the five physical senses is but the finite concept of reality, and in no wise related to the spiritually real, is spiritual sense.

Christ-consciousness beholds God everywhere shining through the mist of personal sense. It recognizes no sinner to be reformed, no sick to heal, no poor to enrich. Spiritual illumination dispels the false concepts or images of finite sense and reveals all being as God appearing.

The light in individual consciousness reveals the world of God's creating, the universe of reality, the children of God. In this light, the mortal scene disappears, and the world of concepts, "this world," gives place to "My kingdom" – the reality of things seen as they are.

Likewise, there is always the sense of an inner companionship. We feel an inner warmth, a living presence, a divine assurance. Sometimes we feel a strong hand in ours or behold a smiling face over our shoulder. We are never alone and we know it. This sweet Presence gives us an inner rest; It enables us to relax from the strain of the world and brings us the joy of peace. In truth, It is a "peace, be still" to every problem or strain of human existence. It is a healing influence within us, and yet It is felt by all those about us.

This inner Presence of which we are aware is Truth Itself interpreting Itself to us as presence, power, companion, light, peace, and healing influence – as the Christ. The consciousness of this inner Being is the result of our greater spiritual illumination, of our cultivated spiritual consciousness. This Truth is the God who healeth our diseases, and It goes ever before us to make smooth our path in life. This Truth is wealth and appears as our abundant supply. No human circumstance or condition can lessen our income and wealth while we abide in this consciousness of the presence of Love.

Establish this truth within you, and it becomes your real being, knowing neither birth nor death, youth nor age, health nor disease – but only the eternality of harmonious being. This truth dispels every illusion of sense and reveals the infinite harmony of your being; it dispels mortality and reveals your immortality. Whatever in your thought is unlike this divine Presence, Truth Itself, must yield in order that you may drink the pure water of Life and eat the spiritual meat of Truth.

To free our hearts from the errors of self – self-will, false desires, ambition, and greed – is to reflect the light of Truth as the perfect diamond reflects its own inner light.

About 500 B.C. it was written: "It easily happens that a man, when taking a bath, steps upon a wet rope and imagines that it is a snake. Horror will overcome him, and he will shake from fear, anticipating in his thought all the agonies caused by the serpent's venomous bite. What a relief does this man experience when he sees that the rope is no snake! The cause of his fright lies in his error, his ignorance, his illusion. If the true nature of the rope is recognized, his tranquility of mind will come back to him; he will feel relieved; he will be joyful and happy. This is the state of mind of one who has recognized that there is no personal self, that the cause of all his troubles, cares, and vanities is a mirage, a shadow, a dream."

So again, illumination reveals that there is no error, that what appears as the snake — sin, disease, discord, death — is reality itself misperceived by finite sense. Then discords are not to be hated, feared, or resented, but reinterpreted until the true nature of the rope — reality — is discerned through spiritual sense. The snake — disease or discord — is merely a state of mind, with no corresponding external reality. It must be understood that no illusion is, or ever can be, externalized.

Spiritual illumination may be attained by living constantly in the consciousness of the presence of perfection, by the continual translation of the visible picture into the reality. We are being faced with discordant appearances all through our days and nights, and these must immediately be translated through our understanding of the "new tongue," the language of Spirit.

Every incident of our daily experience offers fresh opportunities to use our spiritual understanding, and each use of the spiritual faculties results in greater spiritual perception, which in turn reveals more and more of the light of Truth. "Pray without ceasing. . . . And ye shall know the truth, and the truth shall make you free." Translate the pictures and incidents of daily existence into the new tongue, the language of Spirit, and consciousness will expand until translation occurs without even taking thought. It becomes a habitual state of consciousness, a constant awareness of Truth.

Only in this wise can we find our lives unfolding harmoniously from the center of our being without taking conscious thought. Instead of our existence being a continual round of "demonstrations," it becomes the natural, harmonious, joyous unfoldment of good. Instead of repeated efforts to make good come to us, our every good unfolds to view from the depths of our own being without conscious effort, either physical or mental. We are no longer dependent on person or circumstance, nor even on our personal effort. Spiritual illumination enables us to relax our personal efforts and rely more and more on Divinity unfolding and revealing Itself as us.

THE CHRIST

ANCIENT scripture reveals: "Hard it is to understand: By giving away our food, we get more strength; by bestowing clothing on others, we gain more beauty; by founding abodes of purity and truth, we acquire great treasures."

Abraham, the father of the Hebrews, founded the prosperity of his people on the idea of tithing — giving a tenth of one's income to spiritual or charitable purposes without any thought of repayment or reward.

"The immortal can be reached only by continuous acts of kindliness, and perfection is accomplished by compassion and charity." The greater the degree of unselfed love that we attain, the nearer we come to the realization of the universal *I* as our real being.

The personal sense of "I" is busily engaged in getting, achieving, desiring, accomplishing, accumulating; whereas our real Self is giving, bestowing, sharing, and blessing. The personal sense of self is the embodiment of all human experiences, most of which are limited and undesirable: The real Self is the embodiment of infinite spiritual ideas and activities forever expressing Itself without limit or restraint.

The small "I" concerns itself primarily with its personal problems and affairs, enlarging its borders to include members of the immediate family or circle of friends. Personal sense often goes further afield into charitable works or community welfare, but we know that it is personal sense when we analyze the motives which govern. The real sense of Self lives out from the center of its being, blessing all whom it touches, and is recognized by its selflessness, by its unselfishness, by its lack of seeking recognition, reward, or any personal aggrandizement. It is not a spineless entity or a floormop to be pushed around by mortals — it is never even seen or known by mortals.

Two beautiful illustrations come to mind revealing in tender scenes the difference between the personal self and the immortal real Self.

Siddhartha, who had left his home and family in search of truth, finally received enlightenment and became the Buddha, the Enlightened One, or as we term it, the Christ of his day. His father, a great king, was about to die and, desiring to see his son, sent for him, asking him to return. When he sat face to face with his son, he realized that he had lost him in the personal sense of father and son, but tried nevertheless to reclaim him. "I would offer thee my kingdom," said the King, "but if I did, thou wouldst account it but as ashes."

And Buddha said, "I know that the King's heart is full of love . . . but let the ties of love that bind you to the son whom you lost embrace with equal kindness all your fellowbeings, and you will receive in his place a greater one than Siddhartha: You will receive the Enlightened One, the Teacher of Truth, the Preacher of Righteousness, and also the Peace of God into your heart."

The other concerns the great Master. "While he yet talked to the people, behold, his mother and his brethren stood without, desiring to speak with him. . . . But he answered and said unto him that told him, Who is my mother? and who are my brethren? And he stretched forth his hands toward his disciples, and said, Behold my mother and my brethren! For whosoever shall do the will of my Father which is in heaven, the same is my brother, and sister, and mother."

In proportion as we become spiritually illumined, we are sought out by those seeking freedom from various phases of material darkness — sickness, sin, limitation, fear, unrest, or ignorance. We are able to meet these needs only as we impersonalize both good and evil and understand that harmony is the quality and activity of Soul, universally and individually expressing itself.

In meditation or communion, we become receptive to Truth unfolding within us — and this we term prayer. Our prayer should not be connected with a so-called patient. Actually, prayer is not a process, a combination of words or thoughts, nor statements, declarations, affirmations, or denials. Prayer is a state of consciousness in which we experience the realization of harmony, perfection, oneness, joy, peace, and dominion. Often, prayer or communion brings to the individual some specific truth, and this truth appears outwardly as the fruitage of his own consciousness of real being.

It has been revealed times without number that

the talent, ability, education, and experience of every individual is actually Consciousness unfolding Itself in individual ways — as artist, musician, salesman, businessman, or actor. It follows therefore that Consciousness, thus expressing Itself, is never without opportunity, recognition, and reception. Thus there can be no unrecognized gift, no unexpressed talent or ability, no unrewarded effort, since *all* effort and action are Consciousness expressing Its infinite capacities and capabilities. The conscious awareness of this truth would result in dispelling the illusion of unemployment, lack of compensation, or appreciation. Yet — and mark this well — the recitation of these words without some measure of the "feel" of this truth would be as "clouds without rain," "vain repetitions,"— nothingness.

In this same manner, it has been revealed that as there is but one Life, this One is never in danger of sickness, accident, or death. This Life is the life of individual being. It is never necessary to direct a treatment to a person or an animal, but always to be alert and never accept any suggestion in thought of any other presence, power, or activity than that of the one Life, the one Law, the one Soul. To live constantly in this consciousness of good, of harmony, would dispel the illusion of sense whether appearing as a sick or sinful person. The declaration or constant affirmation of this truth would avail us but little, whereas the conscious awareness or feel of it would appear as healing or reformation, renewal, and even resurrection.

Recently, I wrote a friend on the occasion of his birthday and I know he will be glad for me to share with you the ideas that came as I wrote:

"As for birthday wishes, I shall just wish that you didn't have any birthdays so that you could get used to the idea of the continuity of conscious existence without a break or a stop — a conscious awareness of progressive unfoldment.

"Truly there is no break in the continuity of unfolding consciousness, nor can consciousness lose its conscious awareness of body any more than you can lose your consciousness of the developed musical or artistic or other talent you possess.

"Consciousness unfolds from within to the without from a boundless basis or source, from the infinity of your being to the individual awareness of it in infinite variety, form, and expression.

"Death is the belief that consciousness loses its awareness of its body. Immortality is the understanding of the truth that consciousness is eternally aware of its own identity, body, form, or expression. Consciousness, aware of its own infinite being and eternal body, is immortality achieved here and now. The awareness of consciousness maintaining its own identity and form is eternal life. The awareness of consciousness forever unfolding in individual forms of creation or manifestation is immortality demonstrated here and now. This consciousness is you."

Spiritual consciousness is the release from personal effort in the realization that harmony is. This consciousness, with its release from personal effort, is attained as we find the Christ within us a present reality. The Christ is the activity of Truth in individual consciousness. It is not necessarily declarations of truth as much as the receptivity to Truth. As we attain an inner stillness, we become more and more receptive to Truth declaring Itself to us, within us. The activity of this Truth in our consciousness is the Christ, the very presence of God. Truth received and continuously entertained in our consciousness is the law of harmony to all our affairs. It governs, guides, leads, directs, and supports our every activity of daily existence. Where a belief of illness or lack may be, this ever-present Truth becomes our healer and supplier, yes, our health and our supply.

To many, the word Christ persists as a more or less mysterious term, an unknown entity, something rarely if ever experienced by them. This, we must change if we are to benefit by the revelation of a divine Presence or Power within us which has been revealed to us by Christ Jesus as well as by many others. We must experience the Christ as a permanent and continuous dispensation. We must live in the constant conscious awareness of truth active within, maintaining always a receptive attitude — a listening ear — and soon we shall experience an inner awareness. This is the activity of Truth in consciousness, or the Christ attained.

This understanding of the Christ clarifies the subject of prayer for us. The dictionary definitions of prayer all conform to a concept of prayer which is based on the erroneous belief that there is a God waiting somewhere for us to pray to in some manner. Then, if we should find this God in the right frame of mind, we might have our prayers answered favorably; unless of course, our parents or grandparents for three or four generations back have sinned, in which case we would be held accountable for their sins, and our prayer would go into the wastebasket of heaven.

We have a different sense of prayer. We realize that whatever of good comes to us is the direct result of our own understanding of the nature of our own being. Our understanding of spiritual life unfolds in proportion to our receptivity to Truth, not praying up to God, but *letting* God unfold and reveal Itself to us. This is the higher concept of prayer. It is achieved as we take a few minutes now and then during the day and evening to meditate, commune, listen. In quietness, we become a state of receptivity which opens the way for us to feel or become aware of the very presence of God. This feel, or awareness, is the activity of God, Truth, in our consciousness — it is the Christ, the Reality of us.

Ordinarily we live in a world of sense and concern ourselves only with the objects of sense. This gives us our experiences of good and evil, pain and pleasure. As we, through our study and meditation, turn more to the mental side of life, we find that we develop higher thoughts and, therefore, we experience better conditions. As our mental qualities become more refined and we take on more patience, kindness, charitableness, and forgiveness, our human experiences reflect these qualities back to us. But let us not stop there.

Higher even than the plane of body and mind, there is the realm of Soul, the kingdom of God. Here we find the reality of our being, our divine nature — not that body and mind are separate or apart from Soul, but that Soul is the deepest recess of our being.

In the realm of Soul, we find complete tranquility, absolute peace, harmony, and dominion. Here we find neither good nor evil, pain nor pleasure — only the joy of being. We are in the world, but not of it because we no longer see the world of sense as it appears to be but, having awakened our spiritual sense, we "see him as he is" — we see through appearances to the Real.

Heretofore, we have sought our happiness in the objective universe, in person, place, or thing. Now, through spiritual sense, Soul-sense, the whole world tends to bring its gifts to us — though no longer through desire for persons and things, but merely through the avenue of these. In material sense, persons and things are the objectives – that which we desire. Through Soul-sense, our good unfolds from within us, although appearing as person and improved condition. Soul-sense does not deprive us of the friends and family and comforts of human existence, but brings them more surely to us on a higher and more beautiful and permanent level of consciousness.

For many centuries, attention has been centered on Jesus Christ as the Saviour of man, and during these centuries the spiritual sense of life has fluctuated from one extreme to another of light and darkness. A sixteenth century teacher has written: "Christ (Jesus) calls Himself the Light of the world, but He also tells His disciples that *they* too are the Light of the world. All Christians in whom the Holy Ghost lives – that is, all real Christians – are one with Christ in God and are like Christ (Jesus). They will therefore have similar experiences, and what Christ (Jesus) did, they will do also."

Our task is the realization of the Christ of our own consciousness. We acknowledge with joy and deep love the measure of the Christ attained not only by Jesus, but by many spiritual seers and prophets of all ages. Our hearts are filled with gratitude for the measure of the Christ manifested by so many men and women of today. We now look forward to the realization of the Christ of our own consciousness. "The kingdom of God is in you and he who searches for it outside himself will never find it, for apart from God no one can either seek or find God, for he who seeks God, already in truth has Him."

We must understand the word "consciousness" because we can only prove what we are conscious of. Where do we stand in consciousness? Are we still mortals? Or have we renounced our material selfhood and acknowledged ourselves to be the Christ, the fulfillment, the presence of God? Some day we must give up the effort to get and acknowledge ourselves to be the eternal Giver in action. We must feed five thousand without taking thought as to whence it shall come. Out of our Christhood, the multitudes can be supplied. Wherein then is lack except in the belief that we are humans? We must give up this belief and claim our true identity.

When we are confronted with any person or circumstance that appears to be mortal, we must realize, "Thou art the Christ, the Son of the living God," and that all that appears as mortality is illusion or nothingness. We will fear no mortal and no material circumstance because we recognize its nothingness.

Truth is simple. There are no deep metaphysics or mysterious truths. It is either truth or not truth, but there cannot be deep truth and shallow truth, nor can there be degrees of truth. Truth to be truth must be absolute truth. We are concerned now with the truth that we individualize infinite power. We must not look to a power outside of, or apart from, ourselves. We individualize infinite power in proportion to our consciousness of Truth.

The Life which is God is our life. There is but one Life and this is the life of all being, of every individual. We individualize this eternal Life, and it is no less God in one than in another, and it is diseaseless and deathless in all. Our consciousness of this truth is the healing influence within us.

There is but one Consciousness, God. We individualize this omnipotent, omniscient Consciousness;

therefore, our consciousness is the ever-present help in every circumstance. For this reason, we do not pray to, or contact, some far-off Being, but realize the omnipresence of divine Consciousness as our consciousness, and let go of the seeming problem. The awareness of this truth establishes us in the consciousness of the presence of Life, Truth, God. The understanding of the oneness of Consciousness as our consciousness, of Life as our life, is Truth eternal.

The next step in unfoldment is the realization that as the individualization of Consciousness, we embody within our own consciousness our body, our business, and our home. We can prove our dominion over the weather, climate, income, health, and body only as we know these to be ideas of the consciousness which we are. Home, employment, and body are ideas within us and are subject to our understanding, and the consciousness of this truth gives us dominion. This does not exalt humanhood or make it divine: It wipes out humanhood and reveals our divinity.

We can measure our spiritual unfoldment by watching whether or not we are trying to improve the physical scene. We must remember that the structural life of man, animal, or plant is not the one Life, God, but the human, limited concept of real Life; therefore, any attempt to heal, change, or correct the physical universe is evidence that we have not developed sufficient spiritual consciousness.

Christ-consciousness recognizes all life to be God – but realizes that what appears to material sight and sound is not that life, but merely the illusion or false sense of existence. Spiritual consciousness discerns the life which is real.

Inasmuch as we cannot meet a problem on the level of the problem, we must rise above the level of appearance in order to bring out the harmony of being. That which is visible to the five senses is not the reality of things; therefore, we cannot think from that level. Disregarding appearances, we turn from the picture before the senses and begin there to become aware of Reality – of that which eternally is.

OUR REAL EXISTENCE

OUR REAL existence is as Spirit, and only in the degree that we perceive our real existence as Spirit, do we drop the false sense of life as material. Then we see that the structural life of man, animal, and plant is but the false sense of existence; that our concern for the so-called necessities of material living has been unnecessary; that although the beauties we behold all hint at God's creation, they are not that spiritual and perfect creation; that the sick, aging, dying appearances are not at all a part of real life. When we arrive at this state of consciousness, we begin to catch glimpses of eternal spiritual existence, untouched by material conditions or mortal thoughts. As we turn from the world we see, hear, taste, touch, and smell, we catch inspired visions which show forth the earth of God's creating.

In healing work, we must turn from the structural universe which we see. We must remember that we are not called upon to heal it, change it, alter it, correct it, or save it. We are first of all to realize that it exists only as illusion, as the false sense of life. From this vantage point in consciousness, we behold through spiritual sense the "house not made with hands, eternal in the heavens."

We are apt to think of certain people as good providers, good earners, good salesmen, or good healers. Let us understand this correctly. It is never a person, but a state of consciousness, which heals, regenerates, paints, writes, or composes. The state of consciousness becomes visible to us as a person because of the finite concept we entertain of God and man. We often suffer disappointment when some people fail to live up to the picture we have formed of them. This is because we have ascribed the good qualities of consciousness to a person, and then when he fails to live up to those qualities we have erroneously believed to be the person, we suffer.

In the Bible, we meet with the characters Moses, Isaiah, Jesus, and Paul. We should realize that Moses represents the leader-state of consciousness, or leadership; Isaiah presents to us prophecy; Jesus shows forth the Messiah-consciousness, or saving and healing Grace; Paul carries the consciousness of the messenger, preacher, or teacher. Always, however, it is the particular state of consciousness expressing itself and appearing to us as men.

George Washington certainly represents the consciousness of national integrity; Abraham Lincoln, the consciousness of individual integrity and equality.

When we think of ourselves, let us forget our so-called humanhood and human qualities and try to understand what we represent as consciousness and then realize that that consciousness which is expressing itself as us is likewise maintaining and prospering us and our endeavors.

Failure often comes through the belief that we express God, or Life, or Intelligence; or that we express God-qualities. This is never true. God, Consciousness, is forever expressing Itself and Its qualities. Consciousness, Life, Spirit, can never fail. Our task is to learn to relax and *let* our Soul express itself. Egotism is the attempt to be or do something through either personal, physical, or mental effort. To "take no thought" is to refrain from conscious thinking and to let divine ideas fill our consciousness. Since we are individual spiritual Consciousness, we can always trust that

Consciousness to fulfill Itself and Its mission. We are the spectator or witness of this divine activity of Life expressing and fulfilling Itself.

More and more we must become the spectator or witness. We must become the beholder of Life and Its harmonies. Each morning we should awaken with eagerness to watch the new day unfolding and revealing each hour new joys and victories. Several times each day we should consciously realize that we are witnessing the revelation of Life eternal, the unfolding of Consciousness and Its infinite expression, the activity of Spirit and Its grand formations. In every situation of our daily experience, let us learn to stand back of ourselves and see God at work, witness the play of Love upon our affairs, and watch God reveal Himself in all those about us.

Every night we should realize that our rest does not bring to a close God's activity in our experience, but that Love is the protecting influence and substance of our rest, that Consciousness is imparting Its ideas to us even in sleep, that Principle is the guiding law throughout the night. Nothing from without can enter consciousness to defile, and this truth stands guard at our mental portals to admit only reality and its harmonies.

Be a beholder, a witness. Watch the unveiling of the Christ in your consciousness.

There is a constant warfare between the flesh and the Spirit, and this will continue as long as we entertain any degree of corporeal sense. The attempt to bring Spirit and its laws to bear upon material concepts constitutes this war, and peace can only come when the structural sense of the universe and the corporeal sense of man have been overcome.

Notice how often you try to apply some metaphysical truth to a human problem and you will discover the reason for the conflict within you. Our goal actually is the attainment of spiritual harmony rather than a continuation in a material sense of existence with more ease or comfort.

In the early days of our search for Truth, we probably had no other thought beyond making a sick body well, a poor person more affluent, or changing a sinning man into a moral one. There is no doubt but that in turning to a practitioner or teacher of spiritual consciousness we seemed to achieve this end and for some time we continued to "use" Truth, or God, to govern our material concept of man and the world.

It is only as we continue in our spiritual studies and meditation that we eventually become aware of an inner conflict. We enjoy moments of mountain experiences; we tumble into the valley of uncertainty; we achieve victories and then experience failure; we alternate between apparent good and evil, success and failure, spirituality and mortality, health and illness. This is the inner conflict that becomes evident as the warfare between the flesh and the Spirit. This will only end as we drop the mortal or corporeal sense and achieve the consciousness of spiritual existence.

"My kingdom is not of this world" is the foundation for the building of the new and higher consciousness. The willingness and ability to look away from the human sense of person and thing and perceive the man and universe of God's creating is essential.

Gaining more dollars is not spiritual supply; greater savings do not constitute security; physical health is not necessarily a foundation for eternal life: These constitute merely improved human belief.

The advancing student will gradually relinquish

his attempts to improve humanhood or to improve beliefs in order that the truth of spiritual existence may unfold in his consciousness.

The spiritual realm is the source of health which truly is the eternal harmony of being; it is a consciousness of supply without limits and is gained without taking thought. Remember, however, that we are not again connecting God, or Spirit, with the human sense of health and supply. We are rather coming into the awareness of spiritual health and supply. Heretofore, our efforts have been in the direction of manifesting greater harmony and dominion in our earthly affairs. That this consciousness of heavenly being seems to result in more harmonious human living is true, but these are the "added things" which follow the seeking of heaven and its righteousness. The heavenly sense of righteousness will be found to be far different from the human concept of goodness, and it is this higher sense of good we should seek.

"My thoughts are not your thoughts, neither are your ways my ways." For this reason we are not attempting to think more or better human thoughts, nor to have our human ways made more smooth. We truly are seeking to learn God's thoughts and God's ways.

At this state of unfoldment, we realize the need of dropping all concern for ourselves and for our own welfare. We are learning that concern for our personal welfare is building on sand, whereas a life devoted to the search for Truth is a foundation of rock upon which we may build the eternal temple of life. Lasting happiness and prosperity are found when we have a principle or cause to which we can devote ourselves. We are now finding less of self in our existence and thereby making room for the revelation and unfoldment of our divine Self. In this Self, we discover our completeness and the infinity of our being. Here also we discover the reason for our existence.

God evolved the world and all that is therein. What we behold through sense is not that world, but the false and finite concept of the world of God's creating. Rising in consciousness, we begin to perceive the spiritual universe and something of its purpose.

He who has found his inner self realizes that he is one with all men, animals, and things. He knows now that what affects one touches all. The universality of this truth is found in all scripture, as you will note in these examples:

> Let one conquer the mean man by a gift. Charity is rich in returns; charity is the greatest wealth, for though it scatters, it brings no repentance.
>
> HINDU SCRIPTURE

> Theirs was the fulness of heaven and earth; the more that they gave to others, the more they had.
>
> CHINESE SCRIPTURE

> And give unto him who is of kin to you, his due, and also unto the poor, and the traveller. And what good ye have sent before your souls, ye shall find it with God.
>
> TURKISH SCRIPTURE

> It is more blessed to give than to receive. . . . Give, and it shall be given unto you; good measure, pressed down, and shaken together, and running over, shall men give into your bosom. For with the same measure that ye mete withal it shall be measured to you again.
>
> THE BIBLE

As we realize our unity, or oneness, with all creation, we become more loving, gentle, patient, and understanding. Then only are we fulfilling the great teaching, "Love thy neighbor as thyself," and then only are we glimpsing the kingdom of God, the temple "not made with hands" – the man and universe of God's creating. It is this spiritual man, the man of God's creating, who has been given dominion over all the earth.

There is no mystery about the inner life except the mystery of godliness. Every thinker is concerned for his welfare, for the welfare of his family and community, for his country or even for the world. Experience soon convinces him that there is no hope for mankind in the people or the powers of this world. Men are too selfish. On the whole, they are too occupied and concerned with their own interests to be wholly unselfish in their attitude toward the world.

The more ambitious are often endowed with greater physical or mental attainments and soon sit in the seats of the mighty, and the world is led by those lacking integrity and love. Politicians rarely rise any higher than self-seeking, and the occasional statesman is lost in the picture.

Here and there in the world there are those inspired men and women who long for the dawn of the day of the brotherhood of man. Their hearts ache at the constant ridicule of men of good will and at the ever-recurring success of the power-drunk or money-mad in each succeeding generation. These noble people of vision are buffeted between their hope for the progress of mankind and the realization of the futility of overcoming the forces of evil operating in human thought. Eventually the same question comes to each one: Is there no power to stop this reign of evil, to halt wars, to prevent famine and pestilence? Is man helpless before the Four Horsemen?

The search for freedom from the trials and tribulations of human experience has begun. It is really a search for God and it begins at whatever place in consciousness the individual may find himself. If he has a deep religious sense with a church background, he may seek the Power in religious worship, in some creed or dogma or some particular form of worship. The intellectual will undoubtedly seek the Power in the realm of philosophy or one or another of the philosophical religious teachings. In more recent times, the search may turn to the metaphysical church teachings or oriental yoga practices. Without doubt, many go from one to another of these steps still seeking God, or the Power, which may eventually halt the reign of mortality.

One day something happens within. Consciousness expands and sees that which before was invisible. One feels a flow of warmth; a Presence never before known becomes tangible, very real. This often is a fleeting experience. One may not even be certain that it occurred. It lingers in memory, but more as a dream than an actuality, until it happens again, and this time more clearly, more definite, and perhaps lasting longer. Gradually there dawns in consciousness the realization of a Presence always present. This Presence may be felt as if lurking in the background of one's consciousness. At times it becomes a very commanding Presence dominating the scene or experience of the moment.

Now, however, evil is becoming less real; sickness is not so acute; financial stress or even lack gradually gives way to sufficiency; concern for one's self disappears as every need is met without taking thought or planning or worry or fear. The people or powers which heretofore have been feared now fade from view and either disappear from one's experience or else are seen for their powerlessness. Desires become less acute. Fears evaporate. Assurance, confidence, alertness, keenness – these become evident not only to one's self but to those who are met and dealt with in everyday life.

The inner Presence has likewise become an inner Power. From an occasional experience it has become the constant awareness. Forces of pain and pleasure in the outer experience diminish, whereas one becomes conscious of inner powers which are real and which produce and govern the outer life harmoniously and fruitfully. There is no longer fear of the evils of the outer world, nor is there the intense pleasure in the happier things of the outer world. It is possible to have the pleasures of the world and enjoy them, or not to have them and not miss them. There is a constant joy within that needs no outside stimulus.

In this consciousness, God is found to be the inner light or at least this light is felt as an emanation of God. God is felt as a divine Presence or Influence within. It is felt by those who come in contact with the man who has found his inner

Self. It is reflected in his health and success. It radiates from him as sunbeams radiate from the sun.

In finding his inner life, this man has found peace, joy, harmony, security. Even in the midst of a failing world, he stands unmoved, untouched — the very presence of immortal Being.

When we are no longer limited by the five physical senses and have attained even a measure of spiritual sense, or Christ-consciousness, we find ourselves unlimited in terms of "here" or "there," "now" or "hereafter." There is a going in and a coming out without any sense of time or space, an unfolding without degree, a realization without an object.

In this consciousness, finite sense disappears and the vision is without boundaries. Life is seen and understood as unfettered form and limitless beauty. Even the wisdom of the ages is encompassed in a moment. Death disappears, and once more we see those previously separated from us by this so-called impassable barrier. This communion is not the communication as understood in the teaching of spiritualism, but an awareness of eternal life untouched by death. It is the reality of immortality seen and understood. It is a vision of life without beginning and with no ending. It is reality brought to light. In this consciousness, there are no physical barriers of time and space. The vision encompasses the universe. It bridges time and eternity. It includes all being.

In this light, we see without the eye; we hear without the ear; we understand things not known before. Where we are, God is, because there is no longer separation or division. Here there are no rewards and no punishments. Harmony is. Life is not dependent on processes; we do not live by bread alone. *We have the sense of "peeking" into heaven and seeing what mortal eyes were not meant to see.*

Spiritual sense is not engaged with human good, and yet this Christ-consciousness reveals the harmony of being in what appears as our human experiences and in forms available to our present circumstance. Although "my kingdom is not of this world," yet "your Father knoweth that ye have need of these things," and He supplies your wants even before you ask.

And he said unto his disciples, Therefore I say unto

you, Take no thought for your life, what ye shall eat; neither for the body, what ye shall put on.

The life is more than meat, and the body is more than raiment.

Consider the ravens: for they neither sow nor reap; which neither have storehouse nor barn; and God feedeth them: how much more are ye better than the fowls?

And which of you with taking thought can add to his stature one cubit?

If ye then be not able to do that thing which is least, why take ye thought for the rest?

Consider the lilies how they grow: they toil not, they spin not; and yet I say unto you, that Solomon in all his glory was not arrayed like one of these.

If then God so clothe the grass, which is today in the field, and tomorrow is cast into the oven; how much more will he clothe you, O ye of little faith?

And seek not ye what ye shall eat, or what ye shall drink, neither be ye of doubtful mind.

For all these things do the nations of the world seek after: and your Father knoweth that ye have need of these things.

But rather seek ye the kingdom of God; and all these things shall be added unto you.

Fear not, little flock; for it is your Father's good pleasure to give you the kingdom.

Luke 12:22-32

SOUL

THE SOUL is a part of man which is little known and only seldom realized.

Often those in the depths of some deep sorrow break through the mist of material sense to the recesses of their inmost being, where they discover the Soul, or Reality, of being. They become Soul-conscious, and find new values, new resources, new and different strength, and an existence of an entirely different nature.

The exercise of the Soul-faculties results in breaking the illusions of sense. All human discords are products of material sense and are experienced through the five physical senses — that is, all mortal inharmonies are seen, heard, felt, tasted, or smelled. Existing only in this material state of consciousness, discords and disease have their being merely as false sense, or illusion, though naturally seeming very real to the senses.

There are many means of securing temporary relief from erroneous conditions of health, wealth, and other inharmonies of daily existence. Complete and final destruction of error comes only through the achievement and exercise of the faculties of the Soul. The Soul is that part of man which lies buried deepest within him and is therefore seldom realized. We use our mathematical faculties and our musical faculties because these lie nearest the surface of our being, and much more than these, even, our ordinary business faculties and our sense of direction, or even our artistic sense, but artists and authors and skilled musicians go deeper within their being and bring forth the great harmonies of fine music, good literature, paintings, sculpture, and architecture.

Hidden even deeper than these, yet within the reach of our own consciousness, lies the Soul and Its faculties. These Soul-powers, when touched by us, come forth from within us and reach every avenue of our daily life, giving inspiration, beauty, peace, joy, and harmony to each moment of our existence and clothing every event in our experience with love, understanding, and success.

Those too busy with the pains and the pleasures of sense will not, of course, reach the realm of Soul. Throughout the ages the invitation has been extended to mankind to drink of this fountain of living waters, and every generation has produced many men and women who have found eternal youth and peace within themselves. Every so often one arises who has drunk more deeply at the fount of Soul, and these seers have told of the kingdom within and of the life that may be lived through Grace when this consciousness is achieved. On the other hand many answer that they have great human duties which occupy all their time; others require so much time for sense pleasures, pastimes, and recreation; still others are immersed in accomplishing and acquiring.

More and more, people are beginning to realize that freedom from fear, insecurity, want, and ill health is not to be found in the material realm. Wars will not end wars; investments will not ensure security from want. Medicines alleviate pain, but do not produce real health.

Some greater power than can be found in the human body or thought must be tapped to give us the happiness and harmony and peace that are our birthright. This power is available to everyone because it is already a part of our being — in fact, it is the greatest part of our being. As the iceberg reveals only a portion of itself to sight above water, so our human powers of body and mind represent not more than one-third of our powers and faculties.

The powers of the Soul are more real and tangible than any of the material powers of nature or invention. They operate on a higher level of consciousness, but are made evident in so-called human affairs.

Soul-forces act upon the human body to produce and maintain health and harmony. They touch every avenue of daily existence as protective influences and are the source of infinite supply.

The Soul-conscious people of this world live an inner life of peace, joy, and dominion and an outer life in complete harmony with themselves and with all the world of men, animals, and things. They are in tune with their Soul-powers, and this constitutes their at-one-ment with all creation.

Everyone may have access to the Soul. It lies deep within the recesses of our own being. Desire for the higher attainments of life is the first requisite, and then must follow a continuous turning within until the goal has been attained.

A good start may be made through the realization

of the truth that there is more even to human existence than corporeal health and material supply. When we catch a glimpse of the fact that more dollars, homes, or automobiles do not constitute supply, that more travel does not constitute recreation, that absence of illness is not necessarily health, in other words, that "My kingdom is not of this world," we are going in the right direction to discover the realm of Soul.

We all know how to use material force, as when we lift some weight through the strength of our muscles, or exert pressure through arms or legs, and we also understand how to exert mental pressure as in deep thought or through personal will.

That there is a Soul-force we know, but that this Soul-power can do more for us than all the material and mental power combined is but little suspected. Perhaps one reason for the world's lack of interest in this vast subject is that this great reservoir of power resident in our Soul cannot be used for selfish purposes. Think of the enormity of this — a great marvelous power at hand, and yet it can never be used to serve a selfish end. Herein lies the secret of why so few achieve Soul-consciousness.

We only become aware of the presence of the Soul after we have freed ourselves of selfish desires, and in proportion to our desire to serve the interests of mankind do we individualize this infinite power within us.

It is right, natural, and normal that we live full, happy, and prosperous lives, but we can do this without taking thought for ourselves, for our supply, or even our health. All of the good necessary to our welfare will be supplied to us in greater abundance than we can accept when we give up the effort and desire to get, achieve, or accomplish, and come more into the consciousness of desiring only to fulfill our destiny on earth. We are here as part of a divine plan. We are Consciousness fulfilling and expressing Itself in an individual way, and if we will learn to keep our thought away from ourselves and away from the fear that we will be without place or income or health, and let God fulfill Its destiny through us or as us, we will really find all things added unto us.

The Bible is literally true when it says that "the earth is the Lord's, and the fulness thereof" and "Son . . . all that I have is thine." There is no need therefore to take any anxious thought for our own well-being. As we forget ourselves and learn to be a state of receptivity, we will find ourselves filled with Soul-power, Soul-consciousness, Soul-resources, and our lives will be filled with the company of Soul-filled men and women sharing the joys of their discoveries with us.

The mind that was in Christ Jesus is not afar off, nor is it the mind of only a few great religious leaders: The mind that was in Christ Jesus is your mind and it is ready to impart itself to you as you forget self and become receptive to the divine wisdom within you. The resources of Soul are waiting at the door of your consciousness ready to pour forth more than you can accept, but not to satisfy some personal or selfish desire. These false desires are the stumbling blocks to our spiritual development, and we must not think to use our spiritual powers to gain personal and selfish ends. The song of the Soul is freedom, joy, and eternal bliss; the song of the Soul is love to all mankind; the song of the Soul is you.

Why are we so slow in gaining our freedom from illness, discord, and other material conditions? It is entirely because of our inability to grasp the great revelation that there is no reality to error.

So much attention has been given to faith in God to do something for us, or to faith in a healer or teacher, that we have overlooked the great truth: Error is not real—there is no matter, since the substance of matter is really mind.

We are learning from the physical scientists as well as from metaphysicians that what has been termed matter is a misinterpretation of mind. Mind is the instrument of God, and God is Spirit; therefore, all that exists is spiritual substance regardless of the name or nature ascribed to it by finite sense.

God is the consciousness of the individual; therefore, all that can come to us as person, thing, or condition is coming to us as consciousness, in consciousness, and through consciousness; and God, Consciousness, is the Soul of every individual; God, Principle, is the law of all action; God, Spirit, is the substance of all of which we are conscious.

Through false education, which constitutes finite sense, we have come to fear certain individuals, things, and conditions, not realizing that as these are coming to us through the avenue of consciousness they are all God-being, Consciousness-appearing, Spirit-substance. Material consciousness is the false finite sense which beholds the universe and man as limited, as being both good and evil. Spiritual consciousness is the awareness of the individual as God-being, as having only the mind of God and the body of Spirit. It recognizes the entire universe as mind-appearing and governed by divine Principle. Spiritual consciousness is the ability to see beyond the appearance to reality. It is the recognition and realization that as God is our mind, all that appears to us is in and of God which is our only consciousness.

Spiritual consciousness does not overcome or destroy matter or material conditions, but knows that no such conditions exist which finite sense presents. It translates the appearance for us, revealing the true nature of that which is appearing.

Spiritual power emanates from the Soul — the Soul of you and the Soul of me. It is impersonal and impartial. Everyone may open the windows of his Soul and behold the infinite glories of a world far above the universe of sense. Far greater than anything we have ever seen or heard is the world of the Soul, the world that is seen through spiritual sense. We know that unillumined thought beholds the universe as material, whereas the illumined consciousness, or Soul-sense, sees and understands the universe as spiritual.

There is nothing impractical about the development of our spiritual sense or Soul-powers. This uplifted consciousness enabled Moses to lead his people out of bondage and through the Red Sea into the awareness of abundance. Through Jesus, it healed the multitudes of their diseases, fed the multitudes with actual food, and raised the dead. Through Paul, it lifted a portion of humanity above the deepest sorrows and persecutions into Christ-consciousness and spiritual freedom.

Spiritual consciousness lifts us above every human form of limitation and permits us to enter a larger sense of life, health, and freedom. Where there is spiritual consciousness, there is no bondage to person, place, or thing, and there are no limitations to our accomplishments.

So far as is known, Jesus never left a written word, and yet his teaching is the foundation of the morals and ethics for much of the world. Many other seers left only the words spoken to their immediate followers, yet by their own power these messages have become living waters through countless ages. The wisdom of the ages, uttered by spiritually illumined men and women who never dreamed that their thoughts would encircle the globe and influence the lives and conduct of people, is not confined to time or place. The Christlike thoughts that fill their consciousness go out from them like the ring created by throwing a stone in the water, making an ever-widening circle until it embraces all humanity. Yes, spiritual consciousness is practical. Our desire for affluence, however, must be the desire for the other person's affluence before we can experience the grace which is the gift of God.

Meditation is the door to the realm of the Soul, and inspiration is the way. As we learn to take five or ten minutes each morning, noon, and night to sit quietly with a "listening" ear, as we turn within ourselves and learn to wait for the "still small voice," we acquire the habit of meditation and develop skill in its technique until inspiration possesses us and leads us to the haven of our Soul. This is the beginning of our new birth, and here we learn the new tongue of Spirit. Life begins to have a new meaning.

MEDITATION

To MEDITATE IS "to fix the mind upon; think about continuously; contemplate; to engage in continuous and contemplated thought; dwell mentally on anything; ruminate and cogitate."

In the spiritual tongue, meditation is prayer. True prayer or meditation is not a thinking about ourselves or our problems, but rather the contemplation of God and God-activities, the nature of God, and the nature of the world that God has created.

Everyone should take some time daily to retire to a quiet spot for meditation. During this period, he should turn his thought to God, consider his understanding of God, and search out a deeper understanding of the nature of Spirit and Its formations. He should be careful not to take any of his ills or other problems into his meditation. This particular period is set aside, dedicated and consecrated to thinking about God and God's universe.

As God is the mind and Soul of every individual,

it is possible for all of us to be tuned in to the kingdom of God and receive the divine messages and assurances and benefits of the one infinite Love. The grace of God which we receive in these periods of meditation or prayer becomes tangible to us in the fulfilling of our so-called human needs. If we do not open our consciousness to receive spiritual understanding, we must not be surprised if we do not experience spiritual good in our daily living. There is no other way to open our consciousness to the realm of Soul than through meditation or prayer, through contemplating the things of God. "Thou wilt keep him in perfect peace, whose mind is stayed on thee."

All through the day our thoughts are centered on the activities of human experience, on family cares and duties and the earning of a livelihood, on social and community affairs, and sometimes even on the greater affairs of state. Is it not natural then that at some time during the day or evening we take time off to retire to our inner consciousness, which is the temple of God, and there dwell upon the things of God? Above all, we must develop the sense of receptivity so that we can

become ever more aware of the very presence of God in his holy temple which is our consciousness. In the secret place of the most High, which is the Holy of Holies, which is our very own inner consciousness, we receive illumination, guidance, wisdom, and spiritual power. "In quietness and in confidence shall be your strength."

As we learn to listen to the "still small voice," the Spirit of God opens our consciousness to the immediate awareness of spiritual good. We are filled with the divine energies of Spirit; we are illumined with the light of the Soul; we are refreshed with the water of Life and fed with the meat which does not perish. This spiritual food is never rationed to those who learn to meet God within the temple of their being.

To receive the grace of God, we must retire from the world of sense, we must learn to silence the material senses and have audience with God. God must become to us a living reality, a divine presence, a holy Spirit within, and this can only be when we have learned to meditate, to pray, and to contemplate God.

Through meditation, we become aware of the presence of the Christ, and this awareness remains with us all day and all night as we go about our human existence. This awareness enters into our every experience and prospers every endeavor. This consciousness of the presence of the Christ is a light unto our feet and a guiding star unto our aspirations. It is the Presence that goes before us to make the crooked places straight. It is the quality in our consciousness that makes us understood and appreciated by others.

On awakening in the morning, and preferably before you get out of bed, turn your thought to the realization that "I and my Father are one. . . . Son . . . all that I have is thine . . . The place whereon thou standest is holy ground"; and then let the meaning of these statements unfold from within your own consciousness. Gain a conviction of your oneness with the Father, with the universal Life, the universal Consciousness. Feel the infinity of good within you which is the evidence of your oneness with the infinite Source of your being.

As soon as you begin to feel a stirring within you, a sense of peace, or the surge of divine Life, then get out of bed and make your physical preparations for the day. Before leaving your home, sit down and ponder your oneness with God.

The wave is one with the ocean, indivisible and inseparable from the whole ocean. All that the ocean is, the wave is; and all the power, all the energy, all the strength, all the life, and all the substance of the ocean are expressed in every wave. The wave has access to all that lies beneath it, for the wave really is the ocean, just as the ocean is the wave, inseparable, indivisible, one. Note here this very important point: There is no place where one wave comes to an end and the next wave begins, so that the oneness of the wave with the ocean includes the oneness of every wave with every other wave.

As a wave is one with the ocean, so you are one with God. Your oneness with the universal Life constitutes your oneness with every individual expression of that Life; your oneness with the divine Consciousness constitutes your oneness with every idea of Consciousness. As the infinity of God surges through you to bless all with whom you come in contact, remember that the infinity of God is also surging through every other individual on earth to you. No one is sharing anything with you that is of himself, but all that he has is of the Father; so also everything that you have is of the Father and you are sharing it with all the world. You are one with the Father, with the universal Consciousness, and you are one with every spiritual idea of which this Consciousness is conscious.

This is a tremendous idea if you can grasp it. It means that your interest is the interest of every individual in the world; it means that his interest is your interest; it means that we have no interest apart from each other even as we have no interest apart from God; it means actually that all that the Father has is ours and all that we have is for the benefit of everyone else, as everything that they have is for our benefit, and all for the glory of God.

This idea must unfold within you in an original way. It must, bit by bit and day by day, unfold in different ways, and always with greater meaning because of the infinity of Consciousness. You might note how a tree has many branches and how all of these branches are one with the trunk of the tree and, therefore, with the root of the tree; that the root of the tree is one with the earth and is drawing into it all that the earth possesses; and furthermore, that each branch is not only one with the whole tree but each branch is one with every branch, connected parts of one whole.

As you ponder this idea of your oneness with God and your oneness with every individual spiritual idea, new ideas will unfold to you, new illustrations, original illustrations and symbols. By the time you have concluded this morning meditation, you will find that you will actually feel the presence of God within you; you will actually feel the divine energy of Spirit; you will feel the surge of new life within you; and this, too, will lead on to other thoughts.

Whenever you leave one place to go to another place, such as leaving your home for business or leaving your business for church or going back to your home, pause for a second to realize that the Presence has gone before you to prepare the way, and that that same divine Presence remains behind you as a benediction to all who pass that way. At first you may forget to do this many times during the day, but by jogging your memory you will eventually find that this will become an established activity of your consciousness and you will never make a move without realizing the divine Presence ahead of you and behind you, and in this way you will find yourself to be the light of the world.

One of the subjects near and dear to us these past few years is that of peace, but we can have little faith in any perpetual peace based on whatever human documents or organizations can be formulated. True, they have their purpose and they are a necessary step for human beings just as the Ten Commandments were a necessary step until the Sermon on the Mount replaced them with a higher vision. We do not need the Ten Commandments because we need no admonition not to steal or lie or cheat, nor do we need any threat of punishment to keep us honest, clean, and pure; but the Ten Commandments are necessary to those who have not yet learned righteousness for righteousness' sake.

In the same way the world is greatly in need of some kind of a human organization and some kind of a human document to keep some form or some measure of peace in the world. But the real peace, the lasting peace, will only come as it has come to us individually through the realization that we do not need anything that the other person has and, therefore, there is nothing to war about. All that the Father has is ours. What can we want besides that? As a matter of fact, as joint-heirs with Christ in God, we could feed five thousand any day and every day without ever taking thought as to whence it should come.

When all mankind comes into this consciousness of its true identity, there will be no wars, no competition, no strife. As we gain the full consciousness of our true identity, we show it forth in a greater sense of harmony, health, and success, and one by one we attract others who are seeking the same way. In this way all men will ultimately be brought into the kingdom of heaven.

PRAYER

"YE ASK, and receive not, because ye ask amiss," says the Apostle James. Have you ever thought of this when you have prayed for some time, and then found no answer to your prayer? "Ye ask amiss." There is the reason.

Prayer, when based on the belief that there is a need unfilled or a desire unsatisfied, is never in accord with true scientific prayer. A prayer for God to do something, send something, provide, or heal is equally without power.

It is sometimes believed that God requires a channel through which to fulfill our prayer, and this leads us to look outside ourselves for the answer. We may believe that supply can come to us; and, therefore, we watch for the person or position through which it is to come; or we may be depending on a healer or teacher as the channel through which the healing is to come. "Ye ask amiss."

Any belief that that which we are seeking is

anywhere but within us, within our very own consciousness, is the barrier separating us in belief from our harmony.

True prayer is never addressed to a Being outside ourselves, nor does true prayer expect anything from outside our own being. "The kingdom of God is within you," and all good must be sought there. Recognizing God to be the reality of our being, we know that all good is inherent in that Being, your being and mine. God is the substance of our being; and, therefore, we are eternal and harmonious. God is life, and this Life is self-sustained. He is our Soul, and we are pure and immortal. God is the consciousness of the individual, and this constitutes the intelligence of our being.

Rightly speaking, there is not God *and* you, but God is ever manifest *as* you, and this is the oneness which assures you of infinite good. God is the life, mind, body, and substance of individual being; therefore, nothing can be added to any individual, and true prayer is the constant recognition of this truth.

Conscious awareness of our true being – of the infinite nature and character of our only being –

this, too, is prayer. In this consciousness, instead
of seeking, asking, waiting, in prayer, we turn our
thought inward and listen for the "still small
voice" which assures us that even before we
asked, our Father knew and fulfilled the need.
Here is the great secret of prayer, that God is
all-in-all and God is forever manifested. There
is no unmanifested good or God. That which we
seem to be seeking is ever-present within us,
and already manifested, and we need to know
this truth. All good already is, and is forever
manifested. *The recognition of this truth is
answered prayer.*

Our health, wealth, employment, home, and
harmony are then not dependent on some far-
off God, are never dependent on a channel or
person or place, but are eternally at hand, omnipresent, within our very consciousness; and the
recognition of this fact is answered prayer. "I
and my Father are one," and this accounts for
the completeness of individual being.

Properly speaking, there is not God *and* you.
It is impossible to pray aright unless this truth
is understood; and unless we know our real
relationship to Deity, prayer becomes but blind

faith or belief rather than understanding. It is our conscious awareness of the oneness of Being — the oneness of Life, Truth, Love — that results in answered prayer. It is the constant recognition of our life, our mind, our substance and activity as the manifestation of God-being that constitutes true prayer. As we identify this God-being as the only reality of our individual being, we are able to comprehend ourselves as the fulfillment of God, as the completeness and the perfection of being — all inclusive, immortal and divine. The recognition of the divinity of our individual being, embracing and including the allness of God, is true prayer which is ever answered. The correction of the belief that we are ever separate or apart from our good is the essence of true prayer. *That which I am seeking, I am.* Whatever it is of good that I have believed to be separate from me is, in fact, a constituted part of my being. I include, embody, and embrace within myself within my consciousness, the reality of God which forms the infinity of the health, wealth, and harmony of my being. The conscious awareness of this truth is true prayer.

Despite the allness of God, expressed as perfect

individual being, there constantly arise in human experience those ills which call forth our understanding of prayer. What is the nature of error, sin, disease? How can such things be and God be all-in-all? Such things cannot be and are not, despite the appearance of pain and discord and sorrow.

The Bible reveals to us the basic truth of being, namely, that "God saw every thing that he had made, and, behold, it was very good." In this all-good that God made, there is nothing that "defileth . . . or maketh a lie," and there is no other creative Principle. It becomes clear then that that which is appearing as error, sin, disease, pain, and discord is illusion, mirage, or nothingness.

Let us then, as part of our prayer, remember that God made (evolved) all that was made, and in this universe of God there is only the All-Presence and All-Power of God, divine Love, and therefore that which at the moment appears to us as error is a false sense of reality.

There comes a time in our experience when spiritual inspiration reveals to individual consciousness a state of being free of mortal conditions and beliefs. Then we no longer live a life of mental affirmations and denials, but rather receive constant unfoldments of truth from Consciousness. Sometimes this comes through no other channel than our own thought. It may come through a book or lecture or a service imparted by divine Consciousness. Regardless of the seeming channel through which it may come, it is the divine Consciousness revealing Itself to individual consciousness.

As we become more and more consciously aware of our oneness with the universal, or Christ-mind, whatever desires or needs come to us bring with them their fulfillment of every righteous thought and wish. Is it not clear, then, that our oneness with Consciousness having been established "in the beginning" through the relationship forever existing between God and His manifested being, it requires no conscious effort to bring about or maintain? The awareness of this truth is the connecting link with divine Consciousness.

To many, prayer means supplication and petition to a God in a place called heaven. That this prayer has resulted so universally in failure to attain its ends must prove that this is not prayer

and that the God prayed to is not there listening. Human thought eventually realized the lack of an answer to such prayers and turned to a search for the true God and the right concept of prayer. This led to a revelation of truth as understood and practiced by Christ Jesus and many earlier revelators.

Here we learn that "the kingdom of God is within you," and therefore prayer must be directed within to that point in consciousness where the universal Life, God, becomes individualized as you or as me. We learn that God created (evolved) the world in the beginning and that "it was good." Being good, the universe must inevitably be complete, harmonious, and perfect so that instead of pleading for good, our prayer becomes the realization of the omnipresence of good, and so the higher concept reveals prayer as the affirmation of good and the denial of the existence of error as reality.

When the prayer of affirmation results in the use of formulas, it has a tendency to revert to old-fashioned faith-prayer and thereby loses its potency. When, however, one's prayer consists of spontaneous and sincere affirmations of the infinity of God and of the harmony and perfection of His manifestation, one is indeed nearing the absolute of prayer, which is communion with God.

Before our enlightenment in truth, we prayed for things and persons; in other words, we sought to gain some personal end. With his great vision, Emerson wrote: "Prayer that craves a particular commodity, anything less than all good, is vicious." Then this wise man defines prayer for us: "Prayer is the contemplation of the facts of life from the highest point of view. It is the soliloquy of a beholding and jubilant soul. It is the spirit of God pronouncing His works good. . . . As soon as the man is one with God, he will not beg." Prayer must not be understood as going to God for something because, as Emerson continues, "Prayer as a means to effect a private end is meanness and theft."

Now we know what prayer is not, and have glimpsed that prayer is the union of our Self, the individual Soul, with God, the universal Soul. Actually, the individual Soul and the universal Soul are not two, but one, and the conscious awareness of this truth constitutes the union or oneness which is true prayer.

Jesus said, "My kingdom is not of this world," and this we must remember when we pray. To go to God carrying some demand or some desire of this world must end fruitlessly. When we enter our sanctuary of Spirit, we must leave outside all wordly wishes, needs, and lacks. We must drop "this world" and go to God with but one idea – communion with God, union, or oneness, with God. We must not pray to gain anything or to have anything changed or corrected.

Prayer which is conscious oneness with God always results in bringing forth harmony, peace, joy, success. These are the "added things." It is not that Spirit produces or heals or corrects matter or the physical universe, but that we rise higher in consciousness to where there is less matter and therefore less discord, inharmony, disease, or lack.

Communion with God is true prayer. It is the unfoldment in individual consciousness of His presence and power, and it makes you "every whit whole." Communion with God is in reality listening for the "still small voice." In this communion, or prayer, no words pass from you to

God, but the consciousness of the presence of God is realized as the impartation of truth and love comes from God within to you. It is a holy state of being and never leaves us where it finds us.

METAPHYSICAL HEALING

Healings are always in proportion to our understanding of the truth about God, man, idea, body. Healing has nothing to do with someone "out there" called a patient. When anyone asks for spiritual help or healing, that ends his part in what follows until he acknowledges his so-called healing. We are not concerned with the so-called patient, the claim, the cause of the illness or its nature, nor with his sins or fears. We are now concerned only with the truth of being – the truth of God, man, idea, body. The activity of this truth in our consciousness is the Christ, the Savior, or healing influence.

Failure to heal is the result of much misknowledge of the truth about God, man, idea, and body, and this misknowledge stems primarily from orthodox religious beliefs which have not been rooted out of our thought. Few realize to what extent they are blinded by superstitious orthodoxy.

There is only one answer to the question, "What

is God?" and that answer is, *"I AM."* God is the mind and the life of the individual. Any mental hedging or inner reservation on this subject will result in ultimate failure. There is but one universal *I* whether it is being spoken by Jesus Christ or John Smith. When Jesus revealed, "He that seeth me seeth him that sent me," he was revealing a universal truth or principle. There must be no quibbling about this. You either understand this truth or you do not — and if you do not, there is no need for you to seek any further reason for failure to heal. The revelation of Jesus the Christ is clear. "I am the way, the truth, and the life." Unless you can accept this as a principle and therefore as the truth about you and about every individual, you have no foundation upon which to stand. The truth is that God is the mind and life of the individual. God is the only *I*.

Next comes the question, "What is man?" and the answer is that man is idea, body, manifestation. My body is idea, or manifestation. Likewise my business, home, wealth, — these exist as idea, manifestation, or expression. For this reason and for no other, my body is the exact image and likeness of my consciousness and reflects or expresses the qualities, character, and nature of my own consciousness of existence.

So far then, we understand that I am God, that God is the mind and life of the individual, that body exists as the idea of God. God, or I AM, is universal, infinite, omnipotent, and omnipresent; therefore the idea body is equally indestructible, imperishable, and eternal. It was never born and will never die. I shall never be without the conscious awareness of my body; therefore, I shall never be without my body.

When we look out upon the world with our eyes, we are not beholding our bodies, we are not seeing this infinite divine idea body: We are beholding a more or less universal concept of the idea. As we see a healthy body, a beautiful flower or tree, we are seeing a good concept of the idea body, flower, or tree. When we see an aging, ailing body, withered flower, or decaying tree, we are beholding an erroneous concept of the divine idea. As we improve our concepts of idea, body, or manifestation, we term this improving of concepts, healing. Actually, nothing has happened to the so-called patient or his body – the change has come in the individual's consciousness and becomes visible as improved belief or healing. For this reason the healer alone must accept responsibility for healing and never try to shift the blame for non-healing onto the person who asked for help. That individual is I AM, Life, Truth, and Love, and his body exists as perfect spiritual eternal harmonious idea, subject only to the laws of Principle, Soul, Spirit — and it is our privilege, duty, and responsibility to know this truth, and the truth will make free every person who turns to us.

As individual infinite spiritual consciousness, I embody my universe, I embody or include the idea body, home, activity, income, health, wealth, and companionship, and these are subject only to spiritual law and life. The body is not self-acting: It is governed harmoniously by spiritual power. When the body appears to be discordant, inactive, overactive, changing, or in pain, it is always the belief that the body is self-acting, that it of itself has the power to move or not move, to ache, pain, sicken, or die. This is not true. The body is not self-acting. It has no intelligence or activity of its own. All action is mind-action; therefore, omnipotent good action. When we know this truth, the body responds to this knowing or understanding of truth. No change then takes place in the body because the error never was there. It is entirely exchanging a concept for the truth that already is, always has been, and ever will be. Remember there is no patient "out there" and no body out there to be healed, improved, or corrected. Always it is a false concept or belief to be corrected in individual thought.

When we begin to understand that the body is not self-acting, that it responds only to the stimulus of mind, we can disregard so-called inharmonious bodily conditions and abide in the truth that Life is forever expressing itself harmoniously, perfectly, and eternally as the divine idea body.

The understanding that *I AM* individual infinite spiritual consciousness, embodying every right idea and governing it harmoniously, brings forth health, harmony, home, employment, recognition, peace, joy, and dominion. The understanding that this is true of every individual dispels the illusion of hate, enmity, and opposition. This also makes of you a practitioner, a healer, or a teacher, whether or not you are professionally engaged in the work.

We come now to face our orthodox superstitions

and to leave them. Was Jesus sent into the world by God to save it from sin, disease, or slavery? No, God, infinite Principle, Life, Truth, and Love, knows no error, no evil, no sin, and no sinner. Jesus so clearly apprehended this truth that this apprehension became the Saviour, healer, teacher even as it will in you. *The activity of Truth in individual consciousness is the only Christ.* No person is ever the Christ. The activity of Truth in individual consciousness constitutes the only Christ, the ever-present Christ who was "before Abraham." The activity of Truth in your consciousness is the Christ of you. The activity of Truth in the consciousness of the Buddha revealed the nature of sin, disease, and death to be illusion, or mirage. The activity of Truth in the consciousness of Jesus Christ revealed the nothingness of matter; it unfolded as a healing consciousness before which sin and disease disappeared and death was overcome. Every erroneous concept, whether of body or business, health or church, must disappear as the right idea of these appears in individual and collective consciousness.

What about the immaculate conception, or spiritual birth? The immaculate conception, or spiritual birth, is the dawning in individual consciousness of the activity of Truth, or the Christ-idea. It appeared in Jesus as the revelation that "I am the way, the truth, and the life . . . I am the resurrection, and the life . . . He that seeth me seeth him that sent me." The activity of Truth in my consciousness, the Christ of me, is revealing that I am individual, infinite, spiritual consciousness embodying my universe, including my body, my health, wealth, practice, income, home, companionship, eternality, and immortality.

Let the activity of Truth in your consciousness be your first and last and only concern, and the Christ of you will also reveal Itself in an individual, infinite way.

There is no evil. Let us therefore stop the resistance to the particular discord or inharmony of human existence which now confronts us. These apparent discords will disappear as we are able to cease our resistance to them. We are able to do this only in proportion to our realization of the spiritual nature of the universe. Since this is true, it is evident that neither heaven nor earth can contain error of any nature, and therefore the unillumined human thought is seeing error in the very place where God shines through, discord where harmony is, hate where love abounds, and fear where confidence really is.

The work on which we have embarked is the realization that we are individual infinite spiritual consciousness embodying within ourselves all good. This is the song we will sing, the sermon we will preach, the lesson we will teach, and until realization comes, this is our theme, our motif. It is the silver cord of truth running through every message.

Nothing can come to you; nothing can be added to you. You are already that place in consciousness through which Infinity is pouring. That which we term your humanhood must be still so as to be a clear transparency through which your infinite individual Self may appear, express or reveal itself.

When we look at Niagara Falls, we might assume that it would run dry with so much water continually pouring over as the Falls, but looking behind the immediate scene, we see Lake Erie, and realize that actually there is no Niagara Falls, that this is but a name given to Lake Erie at a point where the water pours over a precipice and becomes the Falls. The infinity of Niagara Falls is assured by virtue of the fact that actually the source of Niagara, that which constitutes Niagara, is really Lake Erie.

So with us. We are that place where God becomes visible. We are the Word made flesh. Our Source, and that which constitutes us, is God — infinite divine Being. We are God-being, God-appearing, God-manifesting. That is the true glory of our being.

The story is told that when Marconi was very young, he was confident that he would be the one to give wireless to the world and not the many older scientists who had been experimenting for years. After he had fulfilled his promise, he was asked why he had been so certain that he would succeed. His answer was that the other scientists were seeking first to discover a means to overcome resistance in the air to the messages that would be sent through the air, whereas he had already discovered that there was no resistance.

The world is fighting a power of evil, but we have discovered there is no such power. While *materia medica* seeks to overcome or cure disease, and theology struggles to overcome sin, we have learned there is no reality to disease or sin, and our so-called healings are brought about through this understanding.

We know that there are these human appearances called sin and disease, but we know that because of the infinite spiritual nature of our being, they are not realities of being; they are not evil power; they have no principle to support them; therefore, they exist only as unrealities accepted as realities, illusion accepted as condition, the misinterpretation of what actually is.

We bind ourselves by believing that there is a power outside of us — a power for good or for evil. All power is given to you. And this power is always good because of the infinite Source whence it flows. The recognition of this great fact brings a peace and a joy untold, yet felt by all who come within range of your thought. It makes you beloved of men. It brings you recognition and reward. It establishes you in the thoughts of men and becomes the foundation of an eternal good will.

Whenever you are faced with a problem, regardless of its nature, seek the solution within your own consciousness. Instead of running around here and there, instead of seeking an answer from this or that person, instead of looking for the solution outside of yourself, turn within. In the quiet and calm of your own mind, let the answer to your problem unfold itself. If, the first or second or third time you turn in peace to the kingdom within, you fail to perceive the completed picture, try again. You will not be too late, nor will the solution appear too late. As you learn to depend on this means for the working out of your problems and experiences, you will become more and more adept in quickly discerning your mind's revelation of harmony.

Too long have we sought our health, peace, and prosperity outside ourselves. Now let us go within and learn that there is never a failure or a disappointment in the whole realm of our consciousness, nor will we ever find delays or betrayals when we find the calm of our own Soul and the presence of an infinite Principle governing, guarding, guiding, and protecting every step of our journey through life.

Do not be surprised now when the outstanding truth unfolds to you that your consciousness is the all-power and the only power acting upon your affairs, controlling and maintaining your health, revealing to you the intelligence and direction necessary for your success in any and every walk of life. Does this astonish you? No wonder! Heretofore, you have believed that somewhere there existed a deific Power, a supreme Presence, which, if you could reach It, might aid you or even heal your body of its ills.

Now it becomes clear to you that God-consciousness is the consciousness of individual man; It is the all-power and ever-presence which will never leave you nor forsake you, and It is closer than breathing. You need not pray to It, petition It, or in any way seek Its favor: You need but this recognition leading to the complete realization of this truth. From now on, you will relax and *feel* the constant assurance of the presence and power of this illumined consciousness. You can now say, "I will not fear what man shall do unto me." No more will you fear conditions or circumstances seemingly outside of you or beyond your control. Now you know that all that can transpire in your experience is occurring within your consciousness and therefore is subject to its government and control.

Nor will you ever forget the depth of feeling

accompanying this revelation within you, nor the sense of confidence and courage that immediately follows it. Life is no longer a problem-filled series of events, but a joyous succession of unfolding delights. Failure is recognized as the result of a universal belief in a power outside of ourselves; whereas success is the natural consequence of our realization of infinite power within.

Release from fear, worry, and doubt leaves us free to function normally, healthfully, and confidently. The body acts immediately from the stimulus coming to it from within. New vitality, strength, and bodily peace follow as naturally as rest follows sleep. Little do we know of the depth of the riches within us until we come to know the realm of our own consciousness, the kingdom of our Soul.

When we become still and go into the temple of our being for the answer to some important question or the solution of a vital problem, it is better that we do not formulate some idea of our own, outline a plan, or let our wish in the matter father our thought. Rather should we still the thinking mind so far as possible and adopt a listening attitude. It is not the personal sense of mind, or conscious mind, which is to supply the answer, nor is it the educated mind or the mind formed of our environment and experience, but the mind of God, the Reality of us, the creative Consciousness. And this is best heard when the senses and reasoning mind are silent.

This divine Consciousness not only shows us the solution to any and every problem and the right direction to take in any situation, but being infinite, It is the consciousness of every individual and brings every person and circumstance together for the good of the whole.

Obviously, we cannot look to this universal Consciousness to work with us for anyone's destruction or loss. What is accomplished in and through the kingdom of our mind is always constructive individually and collectively. It can therefore never be the means of harm, loss, or injury to another. Nor do we direct our thought to another, or project it outside ourselves in any direction. That which our mind is unfolding to us, is at the time operating as the consciousness of all concerned. We need never concern ourselves with "reaching" some other mind, or influencing some other person. Remember that the activity of

Consciousness unfolding as us is the influence unto all who can possibly be affected by or concerned in the problem or situation.

There are no unsolved problems in Consciousness, and this same Consciousness which is our individual consciousness is the only power necessary to establish and maintain the harmony of all that concerns us. It is our turning within that brings forth the answer already established. Our listening attitude makes us receptive to the presence and the power within us. Our periods of silent contemplation reveal the infinite force and constructive energy and intelligent direction always abiding in us. Thus we discover in our mental realm our Aladdin's Lamp. Instead of rubbing it and wishing, we turn within in silence and listen — and all that is necessary for the harmony and success of life flows forth abundantly, and we learn to live joyously, healthfully, and successfully — not by reason of any person or circumstance outside ourselves, but because of the influence and grace within our own being.

No longer is it necessary to try to dominate our business associates or members of our family. The law within us maintains our rights and privileges.

Every right desire of our heart is fulfilled now and without struggle or strife, without fear or doubt. The more we learn to relax and quickly contemplate our real desires, the more quickly and more easily are they achieved. It is not required of us that we suffer our way through life or strive endlessly for some desired good—but we have failed to perceive the presence of an inner law capable of establishing and maintaining our outer welfare.

It seems strange to us at first to realize that inner laws govern outer events—and it may at first appear difficult to achieve the state of consciousness wherein these laws of our inner being come into tangible expression. We will achieve it, however, in proportion to our ability to relax mentally, to gain an inner calm and peace, and therein quietly contemplate the revelations which come to us from within. Quietness and confidence soon bring us face to face with reality and the real laws governing us.

Lest the question should arise in your thought as to how a law operating in your consciousness, without conscious effort or direction, can affect individuals and circumstances outside yourself, let me ask you to watch the result of your recognition of the inner laws and learn this through observation.

We are yet to become aware of the fact that we embrace our world within ourselves; that all that exists as persons, places, and things lives only within our own consciousness. We could never become aware of anything outside the realm of our own mind. And all that is within our mental kingdom is joyously and harmoniously directed and sustained by the laws within. We do not direct or enforce these laws: They eternally operate within us and govern the world without.

The peace within becomes the harmony without. As our thought takes on the nature of the inner freedom, it loses its sense of fear, doubt, or discouragement. As the realization of our dominion dawns in thought, more assurance, confidence, and certainty become evident. We become a new being, and the world reflects back to us our own higher attitude toward it. Gradually an understanding of our fellow man and his problems unfolds to us from within, and more love flows out from us—more tolerance, co-operativeness, helpfulness, and compassion. We find that the world responds to our newer concept of it, and then all the universe rushes to us to pour its riches and treasures in our lap.

Many fine treaties and covenants have been signed by nations and men, and nearly all have failed, because no document is any better than the character of those who administer it. When we become imbued with the fire of our inner being, we no longer need contracts and agreements in writing because it becomes first nature with us to be just, honest, intelligent, and kind — and these qualities are met in all those who become part of our experience in the home, office, shop, and in all walks of life. The good revealed in our consciousness returns to us, "pressed down, and shaken together, and running over."

In this new consciousness, we are less angered by the acts of other people, less impatient with their shortcomings, less disturbed by their failings. And likewise, instead of being hampered and restricted by external conditions, we either do not meet with them or else brush right by them with but little concern. We realize that something within us is ruling our universe; an inner Presence is maintaining outer harmony. The peace and quiet of our own Soul is the law of harmony and success to our world of daily experience.

All that has gone before this is as nothing unless you have seen that over and above all knowing of the truth, you must be overshadowed by the Christ.

When the Christ dawns in individual consciousness, the personal sense of self diminishes. This Christ becomes our real being. We have no desires, no will, no power of our own. The Christ overshadows our personal selfhood. We still perceive in the background this finite sense, and at times it tries to assert itself and even dominate the scene. "For the good that I would I do not: but the evil which I would not, that I do," says Paul.

But let it be clear to you that the personal self cannot heal, teach, or govern harmoniously. It must be held in abeyance in order that the Christ may have full dominion within our consciousness.

The work that is done with the letter of truth, with declarations and so-called treatments, is insignificant compared with what is accomplished when we have surrendered our will and action to the Christ.

The Christ comes to our consciousness most

clearly in those moments when we come face to face with problems for which we have no answer and no power with which to surmount them, and we realize that "I can of mine own self do nothing." In these moments of self-effacement, the gentle Christ overshadows us, permeates our consciousness, and brings the "peace, be still" to the troubled mind.

In this Christ, we find rest, peace, comfort, and healing. The unlabored power of spiritual sense possesses us, and discords and inharmonies fade away as darkness disappears with the coming of light. Indeed, it is comparable only to the breaking of dawn; and the gradual influx of divine Light colors the scenes in our mind and dispels one by one the illusions of sense, the darker places in human thought.

The stress of daily living would deprive us of this great Spirit unless we are careful to retire often into the sanctuary of our inner being and there let the Christ be our honored guest.

Never let vain conceit or a belief in personal power keep you from this sacred experience. Be willing. Be receptive. Be still.

SUPPLY

PART I

THE SECRET of supply is to be found in the twelfth chapter of Luke:

> And he said unto his disciples, Therefore I say unto you, Take no thought for your life, what ye shall eat; neither for the body, what ye shall put on.

> The life is more than meat, and the body is more than raiment.

> Consider the ravens: for they neither sow nor reap; which neither have storehouse nor barn; and God feedeth them: how much more are ye better than the fowls?

> And which of you with taking thought can add to his stature one cubit?

> If ye then be not able to do that thing which is least, why take ye thought for the rest?

Consider the lilies how they grow: they toil not, they spin not; and yet I say unto you, that Solomon in all his glory was not arrayed like one of these.

If then God so clothe the grass, which is today in the field, and tomorrow is cast into the oven; how much more will be clothe you, O ye of little faith?

And seek not ye what ye shall eat, or what ye shall drink, neither be ye of doubtful mind.

For all these things do the nations of the world seek after: and your Father knoweth that ye have need of these things.

But rather seek ye the kingdom of God; and all these things shall be added unto you.

Fear not, little flock; for it is your Father's good pleasure to give you the kingdom.

The question now arises: How is it possible to "take no thought" for money when pressing obligations must be met? How can we trust God when year in and year out these financial problems confront us, and usually through no fault of our own? We have seen in these passages from Luke that the way to solve our difficulties is to take no thought for supply, whether of money, food, clothing, or any other form. And the reason that we need have no anxiety about these things is that "it is your Father's good pleasure to *give* you the kingdom" because He "knoweth that ye have need of these things."

In order that we may enter wholly into the spirit of confidence of this inspired message of Scripture, we must understand that money is not supply, but is the result or effect of supply. There is no such thing as a supply of money, clothes, homes, automobiles, or food. All these constitute the effect of supply, and if this infinite supply were not present within you, there never would be "the added things" in your experience. The added things, of course, are those practical things like money, food, and clothing that are so necessary at this stage of our existence.

Since money is not supply, what is? Let us digress for a moment and look at the orange tree which is laden with fruit. We know that the oranges do not constitute supply because when these have been eaten, or sold, or given away, a new crop starts at once to grow. The oranges are gone, but the supply remains, because within that tree, there is a law in operation. Call it a law of God or a law of nature—the name of the law is not too important, but the recognition of the presence of a law operating in, through, or as, the tree is important. That law operates to draw in—through the roots—the minerals, substances, elements of air, water, and sunshine which it then transforms into sap that is drawn up through the trunk of the tree and distributed through the branches and finally sent into expression as blossoms. In due time, this law transforms the blossoms into a green marble and this becomes the full grown orange. The orange is the result or effect of the operation of the law acting in, through, and as the orange tree. As long as this law is present we will have oranges. The orange of itself cannot produce another orange. Thus we understand that the law is the supply and oranges are the fruits, the results or the effect of the law.

Within you and within me, there is also a law in operation—a law of life—and our awareness of the presence of this law is our supply. Money and the things necessary for daily living are the effects of the consciousness of the activity of the law within. This understanding enables us to take thought off the things of the outer world and abide in the consciousness of the law.

What is the law which is our supply? The universal or divine Consciousness, your individual consciousness, is this law. This law actually is your consciousness. Thus your consciousness becomes the law of supply unto you, producing its own image and likeness in the form of those things necessary to your well-being. As there is no limitation to your consciousness, there is no limit to your conscious awareness of the action of the law and therefore no limit to your supply in all its forms.

The divine or universal Consciousness, your individual consciousness, is spiritual. The activity of this law within you is likewise spiritual, and therefore your supply in all its forms is spiritual, infinite, and ever-present. What we behold as money, food and clothing, automobiles and homes represents our concepts of these ideas. Our concepts are as infinite as our mind.

Let us agree now to see that just as we need take no thought for oranges as long as we have the source or supply which is continually producing fruit for us, so we need no longer take thought about dollars. Let us learn to think of dollars, as we do of leaves on trees or oranges, as the natural and inevitable result of the law active within. There is truly no need to be concerned even when the trees appear to be bare, as long as we are conscious of the truth that the law is even now operating within to bring forth fruit after its own kind. Regardless of the state of our finances at any given moment, let us not be concerned or worried because we now know that the law acting in, through, and as our consciousness is at work within us, when we are asleep as well as when we are awake, to provide all those added things.

Let us learn to look at the lilies and rejoice at the proof of the presence of God's love for His creation. Let us watch the sparrows and note how confidently they trust this law.

Let us rejoice when we see the flowers in spring and summer because they assure us of the divine Presence. As we learn to enjoy the beauties and bounties of nature, with no desire to hoard any of them, and with no fear that there is less than an infinite supply of them, so we learn to enjoy the fruitage of our infinite supply – the results

of that infinite storehouse within us — with no
fear of any lack to plague us.

Enjoy these things of the outer realm but do
not consider them as supply. Our conscious awareness of the presence and activity of the law is our
consciousness of supply, and the outer things
are the forms as which our consciousness expresses.
The inner supply appears as the necessary outer
things.

PART II

We say in one breath that we should take no
thought for our supply or for our health, and in
the next breath, we say that we must "pray without ceasing" and "ye shall know the truth, and
the truth shall make you free." Though seeming
to be contradictory, both admonitions are correct,
but they have to be understood.

There is always a belief of human good in
operation — a law of averages, and from this we
derive our material benefit. In house to house
selling, there is usually an average of one sale
out of twenty calls; in advertising through circu-
lars, there is an average return of about two

percent; in automobile driving, it is claimed that a certain percentage of accidents is the rule; life insurance companies have a table of life expectancy, and, from their averages, they can tell you at any time approximately how many years you will continue to live.

To live humanly, that is, to go along from day to day letting these averages affect you, letting human beliefs operate upon you, is not scientific living. This is all a part of the belief of human existence, and unless you do something specific about it, you bring yourself under these so-called economic or health laws. These suggestions, which actually are but beliefs, are so universal as to become mesmeric in their operation, and they tend to act upon those who are not alert, bringing forth limitation.

What must we do to keep ourselves free of these suggestions, so that we can live above them? First, we must live on a higher plane of consciousness. Insofar as possible, we must train ourselves to know that anything that exists in the realm of effect is not cause, is not creative, and has no power over us. This brings up the important point in spiritual wisdom that I am the law, I am truth,

I am life eternal. Since I am infinite consciousness and since I am the law, then nothing in the external can act upon me and be a law unto me. There is nothing from which we can ever suffer but the acceptance of illusion as reality. These things called sin and disease are not what we are suffering from: They are the forms the one error assumes. Regardless of the name we use, they are hypnotism, suggestion, illusion, appearing as person, place, or thing – appearing as sin, disease, lack, and limitation.

We must not live as though we were effect with something operating upon us. Let us remember to live as the Law, as the Principle of our being. We can take possession of our affairs only as we consciously realize that they are the effect of our own consciousness, the image and likeness of our own being, the manifestation or expression of our divine Self – then alone can we be a law unto them.

We must begin our days with the inner reminder of our true identity. We must identify ourselves as Spirit, as Principle, as the law of Life unto our affairs. It is a very necessary thing to remember that we have no needs: We are infinite, individual, spiritual consciousness embodying within ourselves the infinity of good; and therefore, we are that center, that point of God-consciousness which can feed five thousand any day and every day — not by using our bank account, but by using the infinity of good pouring through us the same as it poured through Jesus. We do not meet people with the idea of what we can get or what they can do for us, but we go out into life as the presence of God.

During the day, whether doing housework, driving a car, selling or buying, we must consciously remember that we are the law unto our universe, and that means that we are a law of love unto all with whom we come in contact. We should consciously remember that all who come within range of our thought and activity must be blessed by the contact, because we are a law of love; we are the light of the world. We should consciously remember that we do not need anything, because we are the law of supply in action — we can feed "five thousand" of those who do not yet know their identity.

There is a belief of separation between us and God — our good — and this we correct by realizing,

" 'I and my Father are one'; all that the Father has is mine; the place whereon I stand is holy ground." In the recognition of the infinity of our being, we realize the truth of the Bible, we realize the truth of these promises. They are no longer quotations, but statements of fact, and that brings us to the point of demarcation between "knowing the truth" and "taking no thought."

We are realizing truth now as an established truth within our own consciousness—the truth of our being. We are not taking thought to make any good come to us; we are not giving ourselves a treatment to make something happen to us, but we are realizing the truth, knowing the truth of our own identity, of our oneness with the Infinite, with our infinite capacities. The reason for realizing and knowing this truth is that through the ages we have come to be known as man—as something other than God-being—and unless we now consciously and daily remind ourselves of the true nature of our being, we will come under the general belief that we are something separate and apart from God.

There is a belief that we are separate from some people who are really a part of our completeness,

a belief that we are separate or apart from certain
spiritual ideas necessary to our fulfillment which
may appear as persons, papers, home, companionship, opportunity. This belief of separation we
correct by realizing that our oneness with God
constitutes our oneness with every idea. Illustrative
of this is the telephone. Through my telephone
I can reach any other telephone any place in the
world, but I cannot reach even my next door
neighbor by telephone without first going through
the central station. Then by establishing my
oneness with central, I am one with every telephone. In the realization of our oneness with God,
infinite Principle, Love, we find and manifest our
oneness with every idea necessary to the unfoldment of our completeness.

Never forget that you cannot live scientifically
as man or idea, but that you must realize yourself to be Life, Truth, and Love. You must accept
Jesus' revelation of the *I AM* until it becomes
realization with you.

Stop trying to apply Truth: Attempting to apply
Truth is the action of the human thought. Truth
is infinite; therefore, there is nothing to which
you can apply Truth. It is the reality of being,

and there is nothing inside or outside for Truth to act upon: Truth is self-acting and self-operative.

We are all engaged in activities through which our supply appears to come. Regardless of whether it is a business, a profession, or an art, it is an activity of Consciousness. So regarded, our activity is intelligently and lovingly directed and sustained. It is even more than this: As an emanation of Consciousness, it is Consciousness Itself individually appearing and expressing Its own being, nature, and character. The government is upon Its shoulder, and Consciousness alone is responsible. We learn to let go and let God, Consciousness, assume Its responsibilities.

In the Bible we read of the trials and tribulations of Elijah. As we follow him through the eighteenth chapter of I Kings, we must understand that only the consciousness of the presence of Spirit, God, within him could have done these mighty works. No human power could have accomplished them.

In the nineteenth chapter, we find discouragement creeping in at what appears as the failure of Elijah's ministry. Actually, this was an opportunity for Elijah to prove that the power was not that of a human being, but actually God-power appearing as a man, God appearing as individual being.

The food prepared for Elijah under the juniper tree is his own awareness of the presence of God appearing in tangible form.

We are led in this nineteenth chapter of I Kings to that great message in the eighteenth verse, "Yet I have left me seven thousand in Israel, all the knees which have not bowed unto Baal, and every mouth which hath not kissed him." You note here that God has not saved out seven thousand for Elijah, but for Himself—for God appearing as Elijah.

Whatever our work may be—in business, in a profession, or as an artist—God, the Consciousness of the individual, always has kept seven thousand (completeness) for Himself, and as we learn to listen for that "still small voice" which spoke to Elijah, we, too, will be led to where our work and recognition and compensation are to be found. We exist as individual Consciousness; therefore, all that is necessary to our fulfillment is included in the infinite Consciousness which we are.

In an individual way, God is expressing Itself as you, and your ability is really the ability of God; your activity is actually the activity of

Consciousness, Life; and, therefore, the responsibility for you is God's responsibility. Gain this
consciousness of God's presence and you have
the whole secret of success in every walk of life.

As individual spiritual consciousness, there
are seven thousand (fulfillment) prepared for you
— that is, God, the Consciousness of the individual,
the Consciousness of you, has given you your
individual abilities and capacities, and likewise has
given you the opportunity and the rewards. These
appear to fit each situation.

Always remember that God, your individual
Consciousness, has prepared for you all that is
necessary for the fulfillment of your individual
experience. You are never outside the harmony
of God's being. Cultivate the awareness of the
presence of God every moment.

It is our conscious union with God which
enables us to live without taking thought and
makes possible a life of complete abundance —
by Grace.

There is an invisible bond between all of us.
We are not on earth to get from one another,
but to share the spiritual treasures which are of
God. Our interest in each other is, in truth, purely

spiritual. Our purpose in life is the unfolding of the Spirit within.

From the height of spiritual vision, we do not look upon each other as man or woman as rich or poor, as great or humble. All human values are submerged in our common interest to seek and find the Kingdom within. We see each other as travelers on the path of Light; we share our unfoldments, our experiences, and our spiritual resources. We would not withhold any of these from each other.

Likewise, there is no envy or jealousy of each other's spiritual attainments. Let us even for a moment realize that whatever we posses of supply, position, prestige or power, health, beauty, or wealth is the gift of God and, therefore, equally available to all of us in the measure of our openness of consciousness—and you understand how we can carry our impersonal love out into the human world.

Let us once catch the vision that whatever anyone possesses, even of what appears as material good, is but the expression of his state of consciousness, and it would be impossible to envy another's possessions, or even to desire them. The first step in living by Grace, living in universal peace, must begin with the understanding that all anyone has is of the Father, that is, all that anyone possesses and all that anyone can ever own is the outpouring of his own infinite consciousness.

We are all "joint-heirs with Christ" in God; therefore, we all draw upon the resources of our own infinite consciousness and Soul, and we need not labor, strive, or struggle for that which is already divinely ours. All that anyone possesses at any time, even of what seems to be of human value, is the unfoldment of his own state of consciousness and, therefore, belongs only to the possessor. That which we have is the result of the fruitage of our own state of consciousness; and what we have not yet achieved is our own lack of conscious union with God, our infinite Consciousness.

We can have as much of everything as we desire by enlarging the borders of our understanding and realization. Nothing that we can get from another would ever really be ours, even if we received it legally. It would still belong only to the one with the consciousness of it. What is ours is eternally ours, but ours only because it is our state of consciousness in expression.

All that the Father, my very own infinite Consciousness, has is mine.

The realization of this truth would enable all men to live together in one world harmoniously, joyously, successfully — without fear of one another and without greed, envy, or lust. We would be back in the Garden of Eden. We would live without taking thought, which is by Grace. This would constitute the recognition of life as the gift of God — as the free flow of our consciousness. It would reveal the invisible spiritual tie which binds us in an eternal brotherhood of Love. It would forever solve the problem of supply and thereby establish the reign of peace on earth.

WISDOMS OF THE
INFINITE WAY

BEGIN YOUR spiritual life with the understanding
that all conflicts must be settled within your consciousness.

There is never a conflict with person or condition, but rather a false concept mentally entertained *about* person, thing, circumstance, or
condition. Therefore, make the correction within
yourself, rather than attempting to change anyone
or anything in the without.

Acknowledge God as the substance, law, cause,
and activity of all that is, and immediately
refrain from meddling physically or mentally
in the without. Get back inside yourself, and
there resolve all appearances.

When living out from the center of Being, you are untouched by the thoughts, opinions, laws, and theories of the world. Nothing acts upon you because you do not react to the world of appearances.

In the spiritual life, you place no labels on the world. You do not judge as to good or evil, sick or well, rich or poor. While appearances may show forth harmony or discord, by not judging, you merely know *IS*, and let that which truly *IS* define Itself.

To live spiritually is to know that all is; then do not name, label, define, or judge what is. Be content to know *IS*, and *let* what *IS* reveal Its being, nature, and character to you.

Prayer is the inner vision of harmony. This vision is attained by giving up the desire to change or improve anyone or anything.

Never seek anything or any condition in prayer. *Let* harmony define and reveal itself. Let your prayer be *letting* the *IS* appear.

Prayer is an awareness of that which *IS* by *"seeing"* it—not making it so.

To pray is to *become aware* of the harmony without a mental effort on your part.

Prayer is the absence of desire in the recognition of *IS.*

Spiritual wisdom reveals the deep, clear, cool well of contentment within you through your recognition of *IS.*

Be sure that your prayer is not an attempt to influence God.

Be sure that your prayer is not a desire to improve God's universe.

Be at peace: God *IS*.

Rest in the deep, clear well of contentment within you. Peace already *IS*.

Have no desires in the world. Let God's grace suffice.

There are no powers of evil external to yourself. Discords have no external existence. Resolve them within your own consciousness. "Why do the heathen rage, and the people imagine a vain thing?"

There is an insight in man that visions through all appearances. Be at peace.

Daniel's vision revealed the four temporal kingdoms destroyed by a stone "cut out of the mountain without hands." As you "see" this stone being cut out of the mountain "without hands," you will observe that this stone is the Word. Consciousness, awareness of IS, is the stone which overcomes, without might or power, but by the grace of IS. Be at peace.

IS alone overcomes the world.

The cool, clear water of the well of contentment within refreshes you with the assurance that joy already IS. "Peace, be still."

Take your discords into the well of contentment; wash them, and behold—the grace of God! "My peace I give unto you."

Be not dismayed: "It is *I*."

There are no limitations external to your self. Be free.

Be content with that which is.

Abide in the deep well of contentment. *I AM. It Is.*

If you could discover some form of prayer, meditation, or thought that heals, enriches, or blesses, you would have an *effect* become God. Impossible! Only God is God!

If you could find something or some thought to which to cling—even then an *effect* would be God. Impossible!

It is impossible to realize God as long as one has in mind a "purpose" or "object" other than realizing God.

It is impossible to achieve anything through God as long as one has a desire to achieve it. *God is a jealous God.*

Do not seek in the realm of thought or thing for God.

Anything that can be known is effect—never God. Cease trying.

Men, judging by human standards, complain that prayer is not answered. To benefit by prayer, it is necessary to give up all personal concepts of good. Do not try to fit answered prayer into the mold of human desire.

Truth is infinite; therefore, Truth cannot be known in finite terms.

Go to God as an empty vessel, desiring fulfillment in God's way and measure.

God is not in the human scene. If you were aware of the significance of this statement, you could lay down your life and pick it up again, at will.

Life is not at the mercy of matter.

God is not power. When you reach the center of Consciousness, you find a complete stillness — a deep well of Silence. It is not power, since there is nothing for it to be a power to, or over: *It just IS.*

Gaining an awareness of God does not *produce* harmony. *God's presence is the harmony.*

The only error is the sense of God's absence. The awareness of God does not dispel error — God Itself is the only harmony.

No one can reveal God to another, but by

revealing the nature of prayer, we place him in a position to receive the God-experience. The God-experience can come only through the correct understanding of prayer, since prayer is the point of contact with God; prayer is the avenue of awareness of God; prayer is the preparation of consciousness for the God-experience.

Seeking guidance from God at this stage of your unfoldment will set up a sense of separation from God: It gives a sense of God and *someone* needing help, direction, or wisdom. Actually, *you need to let God be your life* – then It lives, acts, performs, *and IS your very being.*

In our beginning days of meditation, we pondered or contemplated God, the qualities and nature of God, as we understood Him. As we rose higher in consciousness, we learned that any idea of God that we could entertain was not God Himself, but was only a concept of God. Thus we entered the stillness of mind leading to the deep silence of *My* peace – and *experienced* God.

In our student days we sought God, or Truth, as a means to health, peace, security, safety, and harmony. Now we *know* that these are not to be found outside of Him, and that the experience of God is our only desire. Now we have risen above the desire for health or aught save Him alone. All must rise above the desire for peace, health, joy, and abundance. "And this is life eternal, that they might know thee the only true God."

Seeking the objects of good, such as pleasures, things, and places, for the joy of them is a barrier to spiritual unfoldment. Seeking only the realization of God, pleasures, things, and places of joy naturally come into our experience. Then our pleasure is greater in the realization of their Source.

Words and thoughts in prayer are helpful as long as they lead up to the atmosphere of the true communion, which is without words and thoughts. When words and thoughts *alone* constitute prayer, they become a barrier to the attainment of God-awareness.

Do not be misled, here is the secret: Fill your consciousness with the word of God; hear It; read It; ponder It; meditate upon It. This enriches and ripens consciousness, and this deeper, purer consciousness now becomes the cause, law, substance, and activity of your existence. This nobler consciousness which has evolved through study, practice, and meditation attains the conscious communion with God, and reaches through to the deep silence of *My* peace. Then you are lifted into a realm of atmosphere transcending words and thoughts.

The mere reading of truth is but an acquisition of knowledge, not a deepening and enriching of consciousness. *It is the deepened and enriched consciousness which is the Christ unto your experience.*

We do not live on the mortal plane of consciousness where evil can happen.

God is not in the realm or reach of mind or thoughts. You must transcend mind and thought in order to reach God.

Any response on a lower plane than pure consciousness is from one's self rather than one's Self.

O Students! Do not strive or seek for heavenly riches in human consciousness. Wait! Wait! *Seek a higher level of consciousness:* There the Father's treasures are as free as air.

It is a mistake to believe that human desire and prayer will bring God to your side. There must be a rising in consciousness until His presence is attained — and there rest. Here truly is a perennial rest from care, concern, doubt, and fear.

Students are often concerned that their own happiness, peace, and harmony are not complete, that they can bring greater good to others than

to themselves. This often brings doubts and fears
to the student: doubt that God is still with him;
fear that a sense of separation from God may
permanently hold him. *These things come only
that the student never shall be tempted to glorify
himself, or take pride in his own understanding.*

I die hard.

It is impossible to *maintain* a state of consciousness *not attained.*

To assume a state of consciousness *not attained*
is earthly.

Consciousness lives Itself—you do not live It.

Withdraw from personal consciousness as rapidly
as possible. Let "I" die.

Even in metaphysics and spiritual practice, the vision has been on more and larger fish in the nets, instead of on leaving your nets and following Me.

There is no such thing as "my harmony," "my health," or "my supply." *His peace* passeth all understanding. *His* grace is sufficient.

Happiness or unhappiness in human existence, what does it matter? *Happiness must be known of the Spirit!*

Human peace or no peace, what does it matter? *Peace must be known of the Soul!*

Health of the body or no health, what does it matter? *Health must be known of God!*

Wealth of the purse or no wealth, what does it matter? *Wealth must be known of Love!*

In the depths of despair over earthly affairs, this is learned: Find your good in God.

I have told you the *real* secret of life: God is not with mortals. Take it from there.

When the spiritual student's house of cards crumbles, he is near to "an house not made with hands, eternal in the heavens."

Spiritual Student! Rejoice as the outer building tumbles down, for the inner Temple is to be revealed.

The mind of the individual seeking help is the Christ-mind — awaiting recognition.

The man who has his being "in Christ" finds his capacities and abilities in Soul — not in the brain, body, or muscle.

Every action of the organs and every function of the body are the activity of the Soul, appearing as bodily action.

Every skill, every talent, every capacity, and every ability of the mind are really the Soul-action made visibly tangible.

We live in Him. In Him alone we find our completeness and perfection. Apart from Him we are as trees uprooted from the ground — as waves separate from the sea.

Supply cannot be limited since the Soul is its source and infinity.

Soul is the substance, nature, action, and law of *all form and is never separate from the form.*

"Neither circumcision availeth . . . nor uncircumcision." (Galatians 5:2-4; 6:15) This is the Middle Path of The Infinite Way.

Since sinlessness is the opposite of sin, it is not this. Since health is the opposite of disease, this is not it. But — this too is the Middle Path.

The crucifixion of the self is accomplished when there is nothing left for which you wish to pray.

To those unfolding on the spiritual path, come the discordant experiences of human life, until the transition from "this world" has been completely accomplished. The *desire* is to avoid or escape these inharmonies of mind, body, or economic affairs — but this cannot be done, since the discords result solely from the battle with Spirit and "the flesh," that is, with spiritual consciousness and material sense.

To those on the way, harmony in human affairs often is a lack of spiritual awakening; and, therefore, when the battle, leading to the overcoming of "this world" is on, the initiate will remain as quiet as possible under the adverse circumstances, endeavoring to refrain from fighting erroneous conditions and insofar as possible "letting" the warfare go on until the moment of transition arrives.

When your spiritual study is sincere, the breaking-up of your material world — the desertion of friends, students, or family, a change of health or other outer activity — often ushers in the spiritual transition, or rebirth. This is the attainment of that which you have sought.

A tremendous movement is taking place as the initiate discerns the difference between physical harmony and spiritual wholeness.

Retire often into the center of Being, my Son.

Let divine Love engulf you; be at peace in "*My* peace."

Here you arrive at the great experience: the understanding and attainment of *My* peace, *My* wine, *My* meat—the infinite invisible Substance, Law, and Cause.

O my Child! The blessing that is yours as *My* peace descends upon you, and envelops and sustains you!

Now you know the meaning of "*I* will never leave you, nor forsake you." Now you know the rest to be found in the Spirit—that which even the harmonies of "this world" can never give. "Peace, peace, be still."

Santa Claus God! The reason *all* desire is sin is that desire is based on the concept of a giving or a withholding God. Also, desire is based on the acceptance of something or someone or some place other than God.

Since God alone *IS,* and is omnipresence, prayer, true prayer, is a state of consciousness, a conscious communion in union.

I have been in deep grief—so intense that it has torn me to pieces inside—and wondered, "Why, O Lord, why?" In the depth of it, the answer has come: the world's inability to receive and respond to this Christ: the rejection of It by those we expect to possess the gift of vision; the gross ignorance and darkness of the human thought. These bounce back upon me—these rejections and this opacity. Give me Grace to rise above my sorrow.

The Light shines. The Word reveals that when the stumbling block is no longer needed, it is removed. *You* need not move it, change it, or remove it— it is removed when it is no longer needed.

Thank you, Father, for Love.

Truth, as it is usually known or declared, is not Truth, except "in God." When one has attained the *realization* of life in God, it is true that one is spiritual, divine, and God-governed.

Spiritual truth is not true about humanhood, but about Spirit and Its universe. Humanhood is a state of mesmerism, *and only as the illusion breaks* is one's life "in God."

Only "in God" does one attain the realization of perfection, wholeness, completeness, or oneness.

Attainment comes only as one is loosed from all concepts of Truth, and this comes only by Grace.

Divested of all concepts of Life, Truth, and Love, one stands "in God."

Life beyond the grave has no relationship to immortality. Life beyond the grave is but the survival of personality. This personality dies—it must die either this side or that side of the grave—in order that immortality may be realized. *The immortal Self is ever-present,* even when clothed with personality, but is revealed and lived only in proportion as personality, or the human selfhood, disappears.

As long as there remains concern for *personal good*—security, health, or peace of mind—there is that which must "die daily" in order that one may be "reborn of the Spirit" into the realization of immortality here and now.

Prayer is not an activity of the human mind.

All attempts to contact God through the mind or intellect have failed and always will fail. God can be known only through the Soul and the Soul-faculties.

The prayer uttered through the intellect can return fruitage only in proportion to one's belief in that prayer.

Faith in an "unknown God" brings only the harmony of blind belief. God must be known and understood through the Soul.

To an advanced student: You have reached the place where you know every truth that can be known, understood, or received humanly. Now you must reach higher for the Truth that reveals Itself through spiritual means — *without human means of communication.*

Why do advanced Souls, even practitioners and teachers, still experience ills and other problems? Whatever degree of mortal or material consciousness that still remains in them is expressing itself. *There is no unexpressed consciousness,* and even a tiny bit of human consciousness remaining will express itself in terms of human good or evil. This is the law. These two remain side by side until, *in proportion* as spiritual consciousness unfolds, more and more of material sense is uprooted. Even the Resurrection brought forth a material sense of body, with all the marks of human error. In the Ascension, pure spirituality is revealed.

On the spiritual way, many come to barren places—the desert, the wilderness—and believe that God has forsaken them. Often it *appears* as if Christ had forsaken them. Then it is that the spiritual seeker must remember that he has not yet attained, that what he believed to be the full realization of Truth, the Christ, or God, was not the fullness of the Spirit. These wilderness experiences reveal that he must still press on, for when the Light is fully come, "I will *never* leave thee, nor forsake thee." Remember that discords and inharmonies are apparent only to human sense. Spiritual vision sees through—to Reality.

Faith does not concern the past or the future. Faith is an activity taking place in the present—now, only now!

Faith is an activity of consciousness—just as much so as integrity. Faith is always present in you, even though, like integrity, it may be dormant. The recognition and acknowledgement of the omnipresence of faith as an activity of individual consciousness starts the flow of it into visible and tangible effect.

Faith is a quality of God, not of man; but, as a quality of God, it is present in all its fullness.

Do not expect the power of God to function in the "dream," but rather *to break the dream.*

Do not contact God to adjust, change, or heal the dream. The understanding or awareness of God breaks the dream.

To know that one has been functioning in the dream is the beginning of the awakening.

True non-resistance is the ability not to expect God to function in the dream. This does not mean that one lives without God, but rather, one finds his life to be eternally *in God.*

To refrain from seeking the "help" of God is to be functioning in reality.

No longer reaching out to God, no longer seeking God's help is to be awakening out of the dream into reality.

Whenever there is a sense of "needing" God, one is functioning in the dream.

God is not power in the sense of power over evil, sin, disease, or death. God is not power in any sense involving battle, that is, overcoming or destroying.

God is life. God is love. God *IS*. Nothing else is. *Only God IS*.

Do not be concerned about your relationships with people. Consciously maintain your relationship with God, and *this* will take care of everything else.

Keep your realization of your relationship with God sacred and secret. This relationship, maintained in silence and secrecy, appears outwardly as harmonious human relationships and experiences.

God is the cement between you and your brothers and sisters of the human, animal, vegetable, and mineral families.

When thought dwells on person, place, or thing, you are functioning in the dream.

When your thoughts unite in spiritual contemplation, every person, place, or thing becomes a spiritual delight.

The two great Commandments are cosmic law: Thou shalt have no other God or Power; thou shalt love thy neighbor as thyself. Cast *your* bread upon the waters.

"For by strength shall no man prevail . . . . The Lord will take vengeance on his adversaries."

These things we perceive with the five senses are objects of mind, with no relationship to Truth.

All appearances are sense-objects—not of God, or Truth.

All that is objectively witnessed must be understood to be mental images or mind projections—never spiritual reality.

The reality underlies the sense-formation, but is discerned only by spiritual consciousness.

The sense-world—human experience—takes place in time and space, and this in itself precludes its being spiritual in nature.

The universe of Spirit, Truth, God, is an activity in eternity. Thus understood, neither birth, disease, accident, nor death has ever occurred. In every instance, when presented with the appearance of humanhood—even good human beings or conditions—remember that this is not truth, but a mental image in thought, without reality, law, substance, cause, or effect. Then "see" deeper into consciousness and behold that which is— eternity even in what appears as past, present, or future.

If it takes place in time and space, do not accept it at its appearance-value, but search deeper in the realm of the Soul.

THE NEW HORIZON

THE SENSE which presents pictures of discord and inharmony, disease and death, is the universal mesmerism which produces the entire dream of human existence. It must be understood that there is no more reality to harmonious human existence than to discordant world conditions. It must be realized that the entire human scene is mesmeric suggestion, and we must rise above the desire for even good human conditions. Understand fully that suggestion, belief, or hypnotism is the substance, or fabric, of the whole mortal universe and that human conditions of both good and evil are dream pictures having no reality or permanence. Be willing for the harmonious as well as the inharmonious conditions of mortal existence to disappear from your experience in order that reality may be known and enjoyed and lived.

Above this sense-life, there is a universe of Spirit governed by Love, peopled with children of God living in the household or temple of Truth.

This world is real and permanent: Its substance is eternal Consciousness. In it there is no awareness of discords or even of temporary and material good.

The first glimpse of Reality—of the Soul-realm—comes with the recognition and realization of the fact that all temporal conditions and experiences are products of self-hypnotism. With the realization that the entire human scene—its good as well as its evil—is illusion, come the first glimpse and taste of the world of God's creation and of the sons of God who inhabit the spiritual kingdom.

Now, in this moment of uplifted consciousness, we are able, even though faintly, to see ourselves free of material, mortal, human, and legal laws. We behold ourselves separate and apart from the bondage of sense, and in a measure we glimpse the unlimited boundaries of eternal Life and of infinite Consciousness. The fetters of finite existence begin to fall away; the price tags begin to disappear.

We no longer dwell in thought on human happiness or prosperity, nor is there any longer concern about health or home. The "wider, grander view" is coming into focus. The freedom of divine being is becoming apparent.

The experience at first is like watching the world disappear over a horizon and drop down from before us. There is no attachment to this world, no desire to hold onto it — probably because to a great extent the experience does not come until a great measure of our desire for the things of "this world" has been overcome. At first we cannot speak of it. There is a sense of " 'Touch me not; for I am not yet ascended' — I am still between the two worlds; do not touch me or make me speak of it because it may drag me back. Let me be free to rise; then, when I am completely free of the mesmerism and its pictures, I will tell you of many things which eyes have not seen nor ears heard."

A universal illusion binds us to earth — to temporal conditions. Realize this, understand this, because only through this understanding can we begin to lessen its hold upon us. The more fascinated we are with conditions of human good and the greater our desire for even the good things of the flesh, the more intense is the illusion. In proportion as our thought dwells on God, on things of the Spirit, the greater the freedom from limitation we are gaining. Think neither on the discords nor on the harmonies of this world. Let us not fear the evil nor love the good of human existence. In proportion as we accomplish this, is the mesmeric influence lessening in our experience. Earth ties begin to disappear; shackles of limitation fall away; erroneous conditions give place to spiritual harmony; death gives way to eternal life.

The first glimpse into the heaven of here and now is the beginning of the ascension for us. This ascension is understood now as a rising above the conditions and experiences of "this world," and we behold the "many mansions" prepared for us in spiritual Consciousness—in the awareness of Reality.

We are not bound by the evidence of the physical senses; we are not limited to the visible supply; we are not circumscribed by visible bonds or bounds; we are not tied by visible concepts of time or space. Our good is flowing from the infinite invisible realm of Spirit, Soul, to our immediate apprehension. Let us not judge of our good by any so-called sensible evidence. Out of the tremendous resources of our Soul comes the instant awareness of all that we can utilize for abundant living. No good thing is withheld from us as we look above the physical evidence to the great Invisible. Look up, look up! The kingdom of heaven is at hand!

I am breaking the sense of limitation for you as an evidence of *My* presence and of *My* influence in your experience. *I* — the I of you — am in the midst of you revealing the harmony and infinity of spiritual existence. *I* — the *I* of you — never a personal sense of "I" — never a person — but the *I* of you — am ever with you. Look up.

THE NEW JERUSALEM

"THE FORMER THINGS have passed away," and "all things are become new. . . . Whereas I was blind, now I see," and not "through a glass, darkly," but "face to face." Yes, even in my flesh, I have seen God. The hills have rolled away, and there is no more horizon, but the light of heaven makes all things plain.

Long have I sought thee, O Jerusalem, but only now have my pilgrim feet touched the soil of heaven. The waste places are no more. Fertile lands are before me, the like of which I have never dreamed. Oh, truly "There shall be no night there." The glory of it shines as the noonday sun, and there is no need of light for God is the light thereof.

I sit down to rest. In the shade of the trees, I rest and find my peace in Thee. Within Thy grace is peace, O Lord. In the world I was weary—in Thee I have found rest.

In the dense forest of words I was lost; in the

letter of truth was tiredness and fear, but in Thy Spirit only are shade and water and rest.

How far have I wandered from Thy Spirit, O Tender One and True, how far, how far! How deeply lost in the maze of words, words, words! But now am I returned, and in Thy Spirit shall I ever find my life, my peace, my strength. Thy Spirit is the bread of life, finding which I shall never hunger. Thy Spirit is a wellspring of water, and drinking it I shall never thirst.

As a weary wanderer I have sought Thee, and now my weariness is gone. Thy Spirit has formed a tent for me, and in its cool shade I linger and peace fills my Soul. Thy presence has filled me with peace. Thy love has placed before me a feast of Spirit. Yea, Thy Spirit is my resting place, an oasis in the desert of the letter of truth.

In Thee will I hide from the noise of the world of argument; in Thy consciousness find surcease from the noisomeness of men's tongues. They divide Thy garment, O Lord of Peace, they quarrel over Thy word — yea, until it becomes words and no longer the Word.

As a beggar have I sought the new heaven and the new earth, and Thou hast made me heir of all.

How shall I stand before Thee but in silence? How shall I honor Thee but in the meditation of mine heart?

Praise and thanksgiving Thou seekest not, but the understanding heart Thou receivest.

I will keep silent before Thee. My Soul and my Spirit and my silence shall be Thy dwelling place. Thy Spirit shall fill my meditation, and it shall make me and preserve me whole. O Thou Tender One and True—I am home in Thee.

The Writings of Joel S. Goldsmith

LEAVE YOUR NETS
LIVING BETWEEN TWO WORLDS
LIVING BY THE WORD
LIVING NOW
LIVING THE ILLUMINED LIFE
LIVING THE INFINITE WAY
MAN WAS NOT BORN TO CRY
MASTER SPEAKS, THE
PARENTHESIS IN ETERNITY
PRACTICING THE PRESENCE
REALIZATION OF ONENESS
RISING IN CONSCIOUSNESS
SEEK YE FIRST
SPIRITUAL DISCERNMENT
SPIRITUAL HEALING
SPIRITUAL INTERPRETATION OF SCRIPTURE
SPIRITUAL POWER OF TRUTH
THUNDER OF SILENCE
WORLD IS NEW

For more information,
please call DeVorss & Company at 800-843-5743
Or visit our website www.devorss.com